fuss-free
SUPPERS

fuss-free SUPPERS

Jenny Kay & Elinor Storkey

Acknowledgements

The recipes featured in this book are a collection of suppers we have gathered over the years. Some of the recipes have appeared in *The Star* newspaper's 'Angela Day' column and we thank them for the permission to use these recipes. Sincere thanks to the hardworking team at Random House Struik – Linda de Villiers, Cecilia Barfield, Beverley Dodd, Monique Oberholzer and Bronwen Leak – and to stylist Lisa Clark and photographer Warren Heath.

Published in 2012 by Struik Lifestyle
(an imprint of Random House Struik (Pty) Ltd)
Company Reg. No. 1966/003153/07
Wembley Square, Solan Road, Cape Town 8001
PO Box 1144, Cape Town, 8000, South Africa
www.randomstruik.co.za

PUBLISHER: Linda de Villiers
MANAGING EDITOR: Cecilia Barfield
EDITOR: Bronwen Leak
DESIGN MANAGER: Beverley Dodd
DESIGNER: Monique Oberholzer
PHOTOGRAPHER: Warren Heath
STYLIST: Lisa Clark
FOOD PREPARATION: Andrea Maskew

Reproduction: Hirt & Carter Cape (Pty) Ltd
Printing and binding: Craft Print International Pte Ltd, Singapore

ISBN 978-1-43170-007-3 (Print)
ISBN 978-1-43230-060-9 (PDF)
ISBN 978-1-43230-059-3 (e-Pub)

contents

introduction

It's 5 o'clock and it hits you, 'What shall I cook for supper tonight?' We know that today's busy lifestyle leaves few of us with time to spend in the kitchen or supermarket pondering over what to prepare for dinner. It's a challenge to think of something new each day, especially something that will please everyone and result in clean plates all round. We need recipes we can rustle up with minimum fuss, and without the last-minute panic of dashing to the shops.

Having the right tools and a well-equipped kitchen will help you to make more efficient use of your time. Investing in good-quality pots, pans, knives, measuring cups and spoons, a kitchen scale and a few well-chosen appliances will assist with the speedy and efficient preparation of meals. Personally, we find a food processor and a stick blender the most useful pieces of equipment in our kitchens. Organisation is also key, so reading through the recipes carefully and assembling your ingredients will go a long way to quicker preparation of dishes.

A well-stocked pantry is also an essential 'tool' for everyone who loves to cook. It means you always have essential ingredients on hand to ensure the minimum amount of fuss when planning dinners. Try not to clutter pantry shelves with cans and packets of ingredients you may never use. Rotate your stock on a regular basis so that the later 'use-by' date items are at the back, and bring different items to the front so that you try different recipes using other products. This will create variety in your menus and everyone will look forward to mealtimes.

Trust us, we're on your side. Cooking something new and inspiring for supper is going to be fuss free from now on.

Happy cooking!
Elinor and Jenny

A guide to a cook's fuss-free pantry

Most of the pantry ingredients will have a long shelf life, which means you can rely on them to create quick and fuss-free dinners. Here is our list of ingredients we can't do without:

Oils: Peanut oil, sesame oil and sunflower oil for frying and stir-frying. Extra-virgin olive oil for salad dressings. Virgin olive oil for quick, shallow frying and roasting.

Vinegars: Wine vinegar and balsamic vinegar for adding to casseroles and for salad dressings, and cider vinegar.

Dried herbs and spices: Cumin, coriander, turmeric, curry powder, Moroccan spice rub, paprika, cinnamon, garam masala, chilli powder, salt and freshly ground black pepper (*see also* Condiments), bay leaves, juniper berries, allspice, nutmeg, dukka spice mixture and ground ginger.

Oriental and Indian ingredients: Chinese 5-spice powder, green curry paste, red curry paste, fish sauce, sweet chilli sauce, plum sauce, egg noodles, sesame seeds, tikka masala paste, dried lime leaves, oyster sauce, soy sauce, hoisin sauce, ponzu sauce, rice vinegar and laksa paste.

Canned foods: Tomatoes, coconut milk, tomato soup, pineapple pieces, chickpeas, sweet corn, red kidney beans, tomato passata, apricot jam, asparagus cuts, butter beans, tuna in water and lentils.

Condiments: Maldon salt, ground black pepper, black peppercorns, selection of mustards, mayonnaise, tomato sauce, tomato paste, basil pesto, tomato pesto, chutney, gherkins, black olives, Worcestershire sauce, honey, chicken stock, beef stock, vegetable stock, fish stock, tahini and capers.

Dried pulses: Lentils, pearl barley, bulgur wheat and green split peas.

Nuts: Unsalted roasted peanuts, raw cashew nuts, slivered almonds and pine nuts.

Accompaniments: Basmati rice (both white and brown), jasmine rice, all-purpose rice, couscous and pasta rice.

Dried fruit: Apricots, cranberries and raisins.

Alcohol: Red and white wine, sherry, brandy and cider.

Pasta: Selection of pasta such as penne, fusilli, linguini, spaghetti.

Baking ingredients: Soft brown sugar, white sugar, cake flour, self-raising flour, instant yeast and cornflour.

Essential fridge items: Milk, butter, eggs, cream, sour cream and a selection of cheeses (including feta, Cheddar and Parmesan).

Essential equipment:
Food processor – makes short work of slicing, shredding and mixing.
Good micro-plane grater – essential for things such as cheese, garlic and ginger.
Sharp knives – cut through vegetables and meats with ease, making the preparation of dishes quicker.
Stick blender – very useful for blending soups and sauces.

chicken

Moroccan chicken and rice

This is a great one-pot dish with a wonderful spicy flavour.
The dried fruit is optional, but it adds great colour to the dish.

4 chicken breasts, cubed
25 ml (5 tsp) Moroccan spice rub
45 ml (3 Tbsp) olive oil
1 red onion, cut into thin wedges
10 ml (2 tsp) chopped fresh garlic
375 ml (1½ cups) basmati rice
625 ml (2½ cups) chicken stock
5–10 ml (1–2 tsp) salt
100 g dried apricots, halved
1 x 400 g can chickpeas, drained and rinsed
125 ml (½ cup) dried cranberries
125 ml (½ cup) chopped fresh coriander

1. Toss the chicken breasts in the spice rub until evenly coated.
2. Heat the oil in a large frying pan and fry the chicken until browned. Remove from the pan and set aside.
3. Add the onion and garlic to the pan and cook for a few minutes. Next add the rice and cook for 1 minute.
4. Return the chicken to the pan along with the stock, salt, apricots and chickpeas. Cover and simmer for about 15 minutes until the rice is cooked and the liquid has been absorbed. Remove from the heat and stir in the cranberries and coriander.
5. Leave to stand, covered, for about 10 minutes before serving.

SERVES 4

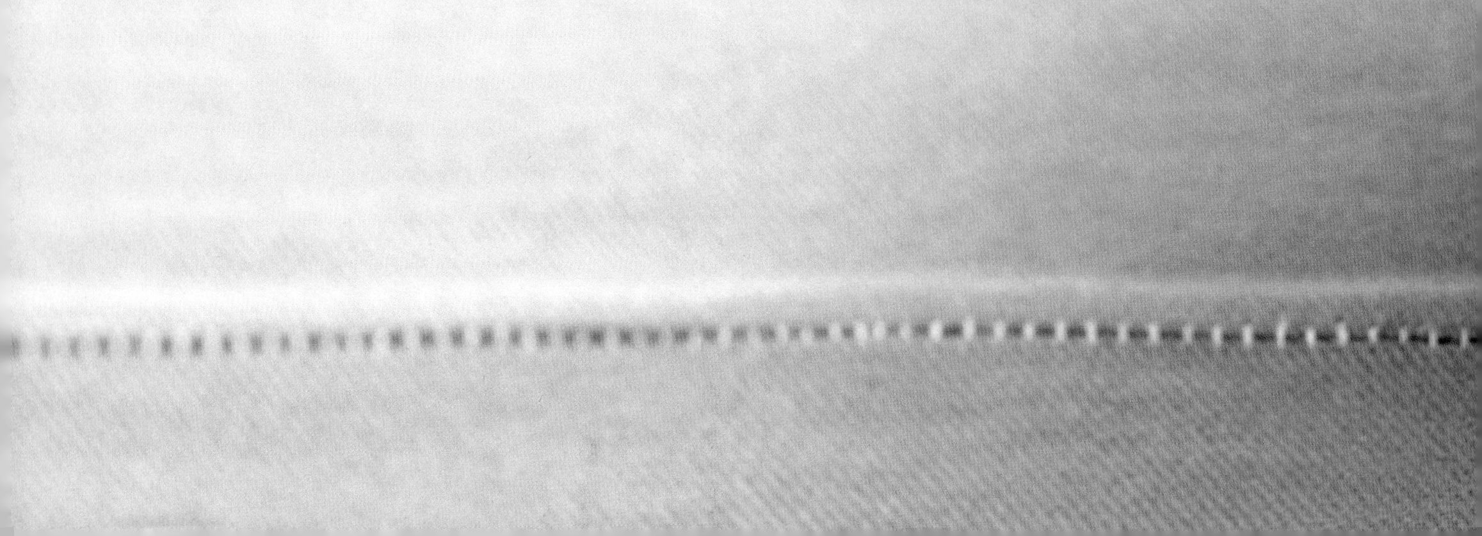

Creamy chicken chowder

The ultimate comfort food.

15 ml (1 Tbsp) olive oil
125 g back bacon, finely chopped
3 large potatoes, peeled and diced
10 ml (2 tsp) crushed garlic
1 large leek, washed and sliced
1 litre (4 cups) chicken stock
3 boneless and skinless chicken breasts, sliced
1 x 410 g can cream-style sweetcorn
25 ml (5 tsp) chopped fresh parsley
125 ml (½ cup) cream

1. Heat the oil in a large saucepan and fry the bacon until crisp. Remove from the pan and set aside.
2. Add the potatoes, garlic and leek to the pan and cook for 5 minutes.
3. Add the stock and bring to the boil, then reduce the heat and simmer for 15 minutes.
4. Add the chicken and cook for a further 10 minutes.
5. Stir in the sweetcorn, bacon, parsley and cream, and allow to heat through. Serve with crusty bread.

SERVES 4–6

Chicken, prawn and avocado salad

This is a perfect, light, midweek dinner and any leftovers can be used for sandwiches the next day.

500 g chicken breast fillets
180 ml (¾ cup) chicken or vegetable stock
1 x 440 g can pineapple pieces, drained and juice reserved
1 butter lettuce or 1 x 40 g pack fresh rocket
1 mango, peeled and sliced
1 avocado, peeled and sliced
150 g cooked prawns
125 ml (½ cup) chopped toasted cashew nuts

DRESSING
125 ml (½ cup) mayonnaise
60 ml (¼ cup) Greek yoghurt
15 ml (1 Tbsp) chopped fresh coriander
15 ml (1 Tbsp) olive oil
1 small onion, finely chopped
15 ml (1 Tbsp) curry powder
15 ml (1 Tbsp) fruit chutney
salt and freshly ground black pepper to taste

1. Poach the chicken fillets for 12 minutes in the stock and reserved pineapple juice. Remove from the heat and allow to cool in the pan. When cool enough to handle, slice the fillets diagonally into 1 cm slices. (Keep the poaching liquid!)
2. Arrange the lettuce or rocket leaves, chicken, pineapple, mango, avocado and prawns on a large platter.
3. To make the dressing, combine the mayonnaise, yoghurt, coriander and 60 ml (¼ cup) of the reserved poaching liquid in a small bowl. Set aside.
4. Heat the oil and fry the onion for a few minutes until softened. Stir in the curry powder and chutney. Remove from the heat and add to mayonnaise and yoghurt mixture. Season to taste.
5. Drizzle the dressing over the salad and top with the cashew nuts.

SERVES 4

Salt and pepper chicken

125 ml (½ cup) cake flour
10 ml (2 tsp) Chinese 5-spice powder
10 ml (2 tsp) cracked black peppercorns
10 ml (2 tsp) sea salt flakes
750 g chicken tenderloins
cooking oil for frying

1. Combine the flour, 5-spice powder, salt and pepper in a large plastic bag. Add the chicken in batches and toss until well coated.
2. Heat the oil in a frying pan and fry the chicken until golden-brown. Drain on paper towel and serve with the mango salsa below.

MANGO SALSA
1 mango, peeled and diced
1 red onion, finely chopped
80 ml (⅓ cup) cocktail tomatoes, quartered
50 ml chopped fresh coriander
50 ml sweet chilli sauce

1. Combine all the ingredients and mix well.

SERVES 4

Chicken and plum stir-fry

Chicken and plum work well together. This dish has a subtle sweet and sour flavour.

30 ml (2 Tbsp) peanut oil
400 g chicken fillet strips, cut into thirds
1 red onion, cut into thin wedges
10 ml (2 tsp) chopped fresh garlic
15 ml (1 Tbsp) chopped fresh ginger
300 g stir-fry vegetables
60 ml (1/4 cup) plum sauce
30 ml (2 Tbsp) sweet chilli sauce
5 ml (1 tsp) sesame oil
30ml (2 Tbsp) fish sauce
300 g egg noodles, cooked
60 ml (1/4 cup) chopped fresh coriander

1. Heat the oil in a wok and fry the chicken over a high heat until slightly browned. Remove from the wok and set aside.
2. Add the onion, garlic and ginger, and stir-fry for 1 minute.
3. Add the vegetables and stir-fry for 2–3 minutes, then return the chicken to the wok.
4. Mix together the plum sauce, sweet chilli sauce, sesame oil and fish sauce. Add this to the wok with the cooked noodles and toss well to combine.
5. Stir in the coriander and serve.

SERVES 4

Satay-style chicken with noodles

We love chicken satay, but it's not always a quick option. Cooked this way, you get chicken in a creamy peanut sauce.

30 ml (2 Tbsp) peanut oil
400 g chicken breast fillets, cubed
1 small onion, chopped
5 ml (1 tsp) chopped fresh garlic
10 ml (2 tsp) chopped fresh ginger
1 red chilli, deseeded and chopped
50 ml peanut butter
250 ml (1 cup) coconut milk
15 ml (1 Tbsp) honey
5 ml (1 tsp) sesame seeds
45 ml (3 Tbsp) soy sauce
15 ml (1 Tbsp) lime juice
300 g egg noodles, cooked
80 ml (⅓ cup) chopped fresh coriander

1. Heat the oil in a saucepan or wok and cook the chicken fillets until browned. Remove from the pan or wok and set aside.
2. Add the onion, garlic, ginger and chilli and cook until fragrant. Return the chicken to the pan or wok, and add the peanut butter and coconut milk. Mix well.
3. Add the honey, sesame seeds, soy sauce and lime juice, and simmer for about 10 minutes until the chicken is cooked.
4. Serve on a bed of cooked noodles and garnish with the coriander.

SERVES 4

Chicken breasts stuffed with goat's cheese and herbs

This dish is simple to make, yet looks impressive and is great for a dinner party. Use herbed or black pepper goat's cheese to vary the flavour.

4 plump chicken breasts
100 g goat's cheese
45 ml (3 Tbsp) chopped fresh herbs
grated rind and juice of 1 small lemon
salt and freshly ground black pepper to taste
250 g streaky bacon

1. Preheat the oven to 180 °C.
2. Cut a slit in each chicken breast to form a pocket.
3. Combine the goat's cheese, herbs, lemon rind and juice, and season with salt and pepper.
4. Divide the cheese mixture between the chicken breasts and stuff the pockets. Place the bacon flat on a working surface and run the back of a knife along the bacon, allowing it to stretch. Wrap each breast with two rashers of bacon and secure with a toothpick.
5. Brown the breasts in a frying pan, then place on an oven tray and bake for 20 minutes. Remove from the oven and rest for 10 minutes before slicing and serving.

SERVES 4

Green curry chicken pies

500 g chicken breast fillets, cubed
30 ml (2 Tbsp) seasoned flour
30 ml (2 Tbsp) cooking oil
1 red onion, chopped
250 g mushrooms, sliced
15 ml (1 Tbsp) green curry paste
1 x 400 g can coconut milk
125 ml (½ cup) chicken stock
grated rind and juice of 1 lime
15 ml (1 Tbsp) fish sauce
10 ml (2 tsp) sugar
cornflour for thickening (optional)
45 ml (3 Tbsp) chopped fresh coriander
45 ml (3 Tbsp) chopped fresh basil
1 x 400 g roll puff pastry, defrosted
flour for rolling
1 egg, beaten

1. Toss the chicken in the seasoned flour.
2. Heat the oil in a saucepan and fry the chicken cubes a few at a time until golden-brown. Remove from the pan and set aside.
3. Add the onion to the pan, along with a little more oil if necessary, and fry until soft. Add the mushrooms and fry for 1 minute. Stir in the curry paste and cook for a further 1 minute.
4. Add the coconut milk and chicken stock, then return the chicken to the pan and add the lime rind and juice, fish sauce and sugar. Mix well and remove from the heat. If you think it necessary, stir in a little cornflour to thicken the mixture.
5. Allow the curry to cool completely before stirring in the coriander and basil.
6. Preheat the oven to 200 °C. Spoon the curry into four individual pie dishes.
7. Roll out the pastry on a floured surface and cut out four large circles to generously cover the tops of the pie dishes. Brush the rims of the dishes with the beaten egg and place a pastry circle over each. Decorate the top with scraps of pastry and brush with the remaining egg.
8. Bake for 15–20 minutes until golden-brown.

SERVES 4

Chicken with creamy pesto sauce

Using plain yoghurt in this dish will give you a lighter sauce than if you use cream.

30–45 ml (2–3 Tbsp) olive oil
500 g chicken breast fillets, sliced
250 g mushrooms, sliced
1 red onion, halved and cut into thin wedges
1 small red pepper, deseeded and sliced
1 small yellow pepper, deseeded and sliced
1 x 125 g sachet basil pesto
175 ml plain yoghurt or cream
salt and freshly ground black pepper to taste
a handful of fresh basil leaves, chopped

1. Heat half of the oil in a wok or large frying and fry the chicken pieces until golden-brown and cooked through. Remove and set aside.
2. Add the remaining oil to the pan and fry the mushrooms, onion and peppers for a few minutes.
3. Combine the pesto and yoghurt or cream and mix well. Add to the pan and cook for a few minutes.
4. Add the cooked chicken pieces to the pan.
5. Season to taste and stir in the basil before serving with basmati rice.

SERVES 4

Chicken curry

Thigh fillets are the ideal cut, as they don't become tough if you cook them too long. You can use breast fillets, but take care not to overcook them.

30 ml (2 Tbsp) cooking oil
800 g chicken thigh fillets, cut into thirds
50 g butter
10 ml (2 tsp) chopped fresh garlic
15 ml (1 Tbsp) chopped fresh ginger
10 ml (2 tsp) ground cumin
10 ml (2 tsp) ground coriander
10 ml (2 tsp) garam masala
5 ml (1 tsp) paprika
1 stick cinnamon
1 x 410 g can chopped and peeled tomatoes
salt and freshly ground black pepper to taste
1 x 400 g can coconut milk
60 ml (¼ cup) chopped fresh coriander

1. Heat the oil in a large frying pan and fry the chicken fillets until brown. Remove from the pan and set aside.
2. Add the butter and fry the garlic, ginger and spices for a few minutes.
3. Return the chicken fillets to the pan, add the tomatoes and simmer until the sauce thickens and the chicken is tender. Adjust the seasoning.
4. Sir in the coconut milk and simmer for a further 10 minutes.
5. Add the coriander before serving with basmati rice.

SERVES 4

Drunken chicken

45 ml (3 Tbsp) olive oil
30 ml (2 Tbsp) butter
2 red onions, sliced
250 g baby button mushrooms, left whole
15 ml (1 Tbsp) cake flour
salt and freshly ground black pepper to taste
15 ml (1 Tbsp) chopped fresh thyme
8 skinless chicken thighs
350 ml chicken stock
10 ml (2 tsp) tomato paste
15 ml (1 Tbsp) grated orange rind
100 ml orange juice
125 ml (½ cup) sherry
15 ml (1 Tbsp) Worcestershire sauce
250 ml (1 cup) sour cream
a sprig of thyme, chopped

1. Heat 30 ml (2 Tbsp) of the oil and the butter in a large saucepan and gently fry the onions and mushrooms for 5 minutes. Remove from the pan and set aside.
2. Season the flour with salt, pepper and thyme, and use to coat the chicken thighs.
3. Add the remaining oil to the pan and fry the chicken until evenly browned.
4. Return the onion mixture to the pan along with the stock, tomato paste, orange rind, orange juice, sherry and Worcestershire sauce. Bring to the boil, reduce the heat, cover and simmer for 30–40 minutes until the chicken is cooked through.
5. Adjust the seasoning, stir in the sour cream and garnish with thyme. Serve on a bed of rice or mashed potatoes.

SERVES 4

Stuffed chicken casserole

100 g cream cheese
60 ml (½ cup) chopped mixed fresh herbs
(parsley, origanum, thyme, etc.)
10 ml (2 tsp) crushed garlic
salt and freshly ground black pepper to taste
8 chicken thighs
15 ml (1 Tbsp) olive oil
12 baby onions
125 g bacon bits
15 ml (1 Tbsp) cake flour
100 ml dry white wine
500 ml (2 cups) chicken stock
50 ml crème fraîche

1. Preheat the oven to 180 °C.
2. Combine the cream cheese, herbs, garlic and seasoning.
3. Loosen the skin on each chicken thigh and spread some of the cheese mixture between the skin and the flesh. Secure with toothpicks.
4. Heat the oil in a frying pan and brown the chicken pieces. Remove and place in an ovenproof casserole.
5. Add the onions and bacon to the frying pan and fry until golden-brown, and then sprinkle in the flour. Stir well until smooth. Pour in the wine and stock and bring to the boil.
6. Pour over the chicken, cover and bake for 50–60 minutes or until the chicken is cooked through. Season to taste and stir in the crème fraîche. Serve with fresh pasta.

SERVES 4

Roast chicken with feta and olives

This is a great throw-together dish, full of colour and flavour.

4 chicken thighs
4 chicken drumsticks
10 ml (2 tsp) paprika
2 red onions, cut into eighths
1 small red pepper, deseeded and cubed
1 small yellow pepper, deseeded and cubed
1 small orange pepper, deseeded and cubed
15 ml (1 Tbsp) chopped fresh garlic
30 ml (2 Tbsp) olive oil
salt and freshly ground black pepper to taste
1 x 410 g can chopped and peeled tomatoes
100 g black olives, pitted
45 ml (3 Tbsp) chopped fresh origanum
125 g feta cheese, crumbled

1. Preheat the oven to 180 °C.
2. Toss the chicken portions in the paprika.
3. Put the vegetables, garlic and olive oil in an ovenproof roasting dish and season well with salt and pepper. Arrange the chicken portions on top of the vegetables and roast for 40 minutes.
4. Remove from the oven and add the tomatoes, olives and origanum. Return to the oven and roast for a further 15–20 minutes until the chicken is cooked through.
5. Sprinkle over the feta before serving.

SERVES 4

One-pot country chicken

1.5 kg whole chicken
30 ml (2 Tbsp) olive oil
30 ml (2 Tbsp) cake flour
1 x 340 ml bottle cider
250 ml (1 cup) chicken stock
1 lemon, quartered
a few sprigs of rosemary, thyme and parsley
250 g baby carrots
300 g baby new potatoes
2 leeks, washed and sliced
salt and freshly ground black pepper to taste
30 ml (2 Tbsp) chopped fresh parsley

1. Preheat the oven to 160 °C.
2. Rinse the chicken under cold water and pat dry with paper towel.
3. Heat the oil in a large ovenproof casserole and add the chicken. Brown very well on all sides. Remove the chicken and set aside.
4. Sprinkle the flour into the casserole and cook, stirring continuously for 1–2 minutes. Pour in the cider and stock and bring to the boil before removing the sauce from the heat.
5. Put the lemon and herbs inside the chicken cavity, return the chicken to the casserole, cover and cook in the oven for 1 hour.
6. Remove the casserole from the oven and arrange the vegetables around the chicken. Season the sauce with salt and pepper to taste and use the sauce to baste the chicken. Recover and return to the oven for a further 20–30 minutes, or until the chicken is cooked and the vegetables are tender. Allow to stand for 10 minutes before serving, garnished with the parsley.

SERVES 4–6

Roast chicken with feta and olives

Marinated chicken flattie

60 ml (¼ cup) chopped fresh mint leaves
60 ml (¼ cup) chopped fresh parsley
60 ml (¼ cup) chopped fresh coriander
5 ml (1 tsp) crushed garlic
60 ml (¼ cup) lemon juice
60 ml (¼ cup) olive oil
125 ml (½ cup) white wine
3 ml (½ tsp) ground cumin
1 red chilli, deseeded and chopped
3 ml (½ tsp) salt
freshly ground black pepper to taste
1.5 kg chicken, butterflied and flattened

1. Process all the ingredients except the chicken in a mini chopper for a few minutes until well mixed and coarsely chopped.
2. Place the chicken in a glass container and pour over the marinade. Cover and marinate for a few hours or overnight.
3. Preheat the oven to 180 °C.
4. When ready to cook, remove the chicken from the marinade and place on a roasting pan. (Reserve the marinade for later.) Roast for 50–60 minutes or until the chicken is cooked through. Alternatively, cook over hot coals.
5. Bring the reserved marinade to the boil in a small saucepan over high heat until reduced by half and thickened. Season to taste and serve with the cooked chicken.

SERVES 4

beef

Pepper steak with mushrooms

A family favourite reserved for special occasions; use mixed peppercorns for a variation.

15 ml (1 Tbsp) black peppercorns, crushed
4 rump or sirloin steaks
15 ml (1 Tbsp) olive oil
salt to taste
60 g butter
250 g mushrooms, sliced
5 ml (1 tsp) chopped fresh garlic
10 ml (2 tsp) cake flour
10 ml (2 tsp) Worcestershire sauce
45 ml (3 Tbsp) lemon juice
125 ml (½ cup) cream
15 ml (1 Tbsp) brandy
roasted vine tomatoes to garnish (optional)

1. Press the crushed peppercorns into the steaks.
2. Heat the oil in a frying pan and cook the steaks until done to your liking. Season with salt, remove from the pan and set aside, covered with foil.
3. Add the butter to the pan and cook the mushrooms and garlic until soft.
4. Stir in the flour and cook for 1 minute, then add the Worcestershire sauce, lemon juice and cream, and bring to the boil stirring until thickened. Stir in the brandy.
5. Pour over the steaks or serve on the side. If you like, garnish with roasted vine tomatoes.These steaks are delicious served with mashed potatoes or French fries.

SERVES 4

Asian beef salad

This dish will stretch your meat. It is also excellent made with ostrich steak.

600 g rump or sirloin steak
30 ml (2 Tbsp) olive oil
1 pillow pkt lettuce leaves
½ red pepper, deseeded and diced
½ yellow pepper, deseeded and diced
½ red onion, thinly sliced
125 g cocktail tomatoes, halved
½ English cucumber, deseeded and sliced
a handful of fresh coriander

DRESSING
60 ml (¼ cup) lime juice
30 ml (2 Tbsp) sweet chilli sauce
30 ml (2 Tbsp) fish sauce
10 ml (2 tsp) chopped fresh garlic
15 ml (1 Tbsp) honey
5 ml (1 tsp) sesame oil

1. Brush the steaks with the oil and cook on a griddle pan until done to your liking. Set aside to cool slightly before slicing into strips.
2. To make the dressing, combine all the ingredients in a screw-top jar and shake well.
3. Pour half of the dressing over the steak and set aside for about 30 minutes.
4. In a serving bowl, toss together the steak slices, lettuce, peppers, onion, tomatoes, cucumber and coriander. Pour over the remaining dressing and serve.

SERVES 4

Hearty beef and vegetable soup

This warming dish is a meal on its own and perfect for a cold winter's night.

45 ml (3 Tbsp) olive oil
1 kg blade beef, cubed
2 cloves garlic, crushed
2 onions, chopped
250 ml (1 cup) pearl barley
1 litre (4 cups) beef stock
1.5 litres (6 cups) water
2 bay leaves
5 ml (1 tsp) chopped fresh thyme leaves
2 potatoes, peeled and cubed
2 carrots, peeled and diced
salt and freshly ground black pepper to taste
a few sprigs of fresh rosemary

1. Heat the oil in a large saucepan and brown the beef in batches. Set aside.
2. Add the garlic and onions to the pan and cook until soft over a medium heat.
3. Return the meat to the pan, and add the barley, stock, water and herbs. Cover and simmer for about 1 hour.
4. Add the potatoes and carrots, and simmer until the vegetables are soft and the meat tender. Add more stock if the soup seems too thick.
5. Remove from the heat, discard the bay leaves and season well. Serve in bowls garnished with sprigs of rosemary.

SERVES 4–6

Beef and pepper noodles

All cooked in one pan, this is simple and super fast.

30 ml (2 Tbsp) oil
1 orange or yellow pepper, deseeded and sliced
1 onion, sliced
500 g rump steak, sliced into thin strips
600 g bok choy or baby spinach
2 x 150 g packs pre-cooked egg noodles

STIR-FRY SAUCE
5 ml (1 tsp) grated fresh ginger
5 ml (1 tsp) chopped fresh garlic
125 ml (½ cup) mild sweet chilli sauce
60 ml (¼ cup) hoisin sauce
30 ml (2 Tbsp) soy sauce
15 ml (1 Tbsp) fish sauce

1. Make the sauce by mixing all the ingredients together.
2. Heat the oil in a wok or large frying pan and cook the pepper and onion quickly for 1 minute.
3. Add the beef and fry until well browned.
4. Add the bok choy or spinach and cook briefly until it begins to wilt.
5. Stir in the sauce, bring to the boil and add the noodles. Cook for a further 2 minutes, loosening the noodles until they are coated in the sauce. Serve immediately.

Note: A store-bought stir-fry sauce can be used instead.

SERVES 4

Beef and broccoli stir-fry

Make sure your wok is really hot when cooking the steak and take care not to add too much meat at once as this will lower the temperature of the wok and cause the meat to stew instead of stir-fry quickly.

30 ml (2 Tbsp) peanut oil
500 g rump or sirloin steak, sliced into strips
1 red onion, cut into thin wedges
250 g broccoli florets
125 g green beans, cut into 2 cm pieces
60 ml (¼ cup) tomato sauce
30 ml (2 Tbsp) soy sauce
30 ml (2 Tbsp) oyster sauce
45 ml (3 Tbsp) sweet chilli sauce
5 ml (1 tsp) sesame oil
30 ml (2 Tbsp) sherry
5 ml (1 tsp) chopped fresh garlic
5 ml (1 tsp) chopped fresh ginger
300 g egg noodles, soaked and drained (optional)
60 ml (¼ cup) chopped fresh coriander

1. Heat the peanut oil in a wok and cook the meat in batches over a high heat until browned. Remove and set aside.
2. Add a little more oil to the wok and fry the onion, broccoli and beans until just tender. Return the meat to the wok.
3. Combine the tomato sauce, soy sauce, oyster sauce, sweet chilli sauce, sesame oil, sherry, garlic and ginger, and add this to the wok. Toss well to combine.
4. If using, add the noodles and stir to coat with the sauce. Sprinkle with the coriander and serve immediately.

SERVES 4

Stir-fry beef with cashews

This recipe also works well with ostrich steaks. It is important not to overcook ostrich, as it tends to become tough. Instead of serving the dish over noodles, try folding the noodles into the dish so that they soak up the lovely sauce.

30 ml (2 Tbsp) peanut oil
500 g rump steak, cut into thin slices
1 onion, cut into thin wedges
1 red pepper, deseeded and sliced
125 g broccoli florets
10 ml (2 tsp) chopped fresh garlic
10 ml (2 tsp) grated fresh ginger
1–2 green chillies, deseeded and chopped
60 ml (¼ cup) hoisin sauce
45 ml (3 Tbsp) oyster sauce
30 ml (2 Tbsp) soy sauce
50 g toasted whole cashew nuts
a handful of chopped fresh coriander
rice or egg noodles to serve

1. Heat half of the oil in a large wok over a high heat. Add the meat in batches and cook quickly until well browned. Remove from the wok and set aside.
2. Heat the remaining oil in the wok over a medium–high heat. Add the onion, red pepper, broccoli, garlic, ginger and chilli. Cook, tossing continuously, for 3–4 minutes or until the vegetables are just tender. Return the meat to the wok.
3. Combine the hoisin sauce, oyster sauce and soy sauce, and add to the wok. Toss until well combined and heated through.
4. Scatter over the cashews and serve, sprinkled with coriander, over rice or noodles.

SERVES 4

Beef burgers

These are quick and easy to prepare. Those that aren't used can be frozen for another day.

500 g lean beef mince
125 ml (½ cup) breadcrumbs made from day-old bread
10 ml (2 tsp) crushed garlic
1 onion, grated
15 ml (1 Tbsp) Worcestershire sauce
15 ml (1 Tbsp) tomato pesto
1 egg
1 large carrot, peeled and grated
salt and freshly ground black pepper to taste
oil for frying

FOR SERVING
8 rolls, toasted and buttered
lettuce or rocket leaves
sliced tomato (optional)
sliced gherkin (optional)
thinly sliced onion (optional)

1. Combine all the ingredients except the oil and shape the mixture into eight patties. Cover with clingfilm and refrigerate for at least 30 minutes before cooking. (Chilling helps hold them together when cooking.)
2. Preheat the oil in a large frying pan over a medium heat.
3. Cook the patties for 4–5 minutes on each side, or until browned and cooked through. Don't press down on the meat, as this will squeeze out the juices. If you like your burgers pink in the middle, cook for 3–4 minutes on each side.
4. Transfer the cooked patties to an ovenproof dish, cover and keep warm while you cook the remaining patties.
5. Serve on toasted, buttered rolls garnished with lettuce or rocket and your choice of sliced tomato, gherkin and onion.

MAKES 8 BURGERS

Beef and lentil curry

Take care not to cook the steak too long as it will become tough. It is better to undercook it slightly in the beginning, as it will finish cooking when you reheat it.

30 ml (2 Tbsp) cooking oil
700 g beef steak, cut into 2 cm cubes
1 onion, chopped
10 ml (2 tsp) chopped fresh garlic
10 ml (2 tsp) chopped fresh ginger
45 ml (3 Tbsp) tikka masala curry paste
250 ml (1 cup) red lentils
250 ml (1 cup) beef stock
1 x 400 g can coconut milk
125 ml (½ cup) water
salt and freshly ground black pepper to taste
60 ml (¼ cup) chopped fresh coriander

1. Heat the oil in a large saucepan and fry the beef quickly until browned. Remove from the pan and set aside.
2. Add the onion, garlic, ginger and curry paste to the pan and cook until the onion has softened.
3. Add the lentils, stock, coconut milk and water, and simmer, uncovered, stirring frequently for 10–15 minutes until the lentils are soft and the mixture has thickened.
4. Return the beef to the pan and cook for about 5 minutes. Season to taste and mix in the coriander. Serve with basmati rice.

SERVES 4

Red beef curry

A good way to make a small amount of fillet steak s-t-r-e-t-c-h a long way.

1 x 400 g can coconut milk
15–30 ml (1–2 Tbsp) red curry paste
30 ml (2 Tbsp) fish sauce
45 ml (3 Tbsp) palm sugar
500 g fillet steak, cut into stir-fry strips
250 g baby button mushrooms
6 fresh (or 3 dried) lime leaves
1 red chilli, finely chopped
125 ml (½ cup) ground roasted unsalted peanuts
extra chopped red chilli and fresh lime leaves

1. Pour half of the coconut milk into a wok and heat on medium. Add the curry paste, stir well to combine and bring to the boil. Cook for a few minutes until fragrant.
2. Stir in the fish sauce and palm sugar and cook for a further few minutes.
3. Add the meat and cook for 5 minutes, and then add the mushrooms.
4. Pour in the remaining coconut milk, and add the lime leaves, chilli and peanuts. Simmer for 10 minutes.
5. Spoon into a serving dish and sprinkle over some extra chopped chilli and garnish with lime leaves.

SERVES 4–6

Fuss-free beef curry

To save time, ready-cubed stewing beef can be used. This is a good recipe for a slow cooker.

1 kg beef shin, cubed
60 ml (¼ cup) seasoned flour
45 ml (3 Tbsp) cooking oil
2 onions, chopped
10 ml (2 tsp) chopped fresh ginger
10 ml (2 tsp) chopped fresh garlic
10 ml (2 tsp) ground coriander
10 ml (2 tsp) ground cumin
5 ml (1 tsp) ground cinnamon
10 ml (2 tsp) mild curry powder
5 ml (1 tsp) turmeric
3 ml (½ tsp) ground cloves
3 ml (½ tsp) ground allspice
1 x 410 g can chopped and peeled tomatoes
500 ml (2 cups) beef stock
2–3 carrots, peeled and chopped
2–3 potatoes, peeled and diced
15 ml (1 Tbsp) sugar
salt and freshly ground black pepper to taste

1. Toss the beef cubes in the seasoned flour.
2. Heat the oil in a large saucepan and fry the beef in batches until nicely browned. Remove from the pan and set aside.
3. Add the onions to the pan and fry gently until soft. Add the ginger and garlic and fry for 1 minute. Add all the spices and fry until fragrant, then return the meat to the pan and stir to coat.
4. Add the tomatoes and stock and bring to the boil Add the carrots, potatoes and sugar. Season with salt and pepper and simmer covered for 2–3 hours until the meat is tender. Serve with rice.

SERVES 4

Beef and brinjal pie

If the brinjal is fresh and firm you can skip the salting step as it probably won't be bitter.

1 large brinjal, diced
30 ml (2 Tbsp) olive oil
1 onion, chopped
10 ml (2 tsp) chopped fresh garlic
500 g beef mince
10 ml (2 tsp) ground cumin
10 ml (2 tsp) ground coriander
1 stick cinnamon
15 ml (1 Tbsp) tomato paste
1 x 410 g can chopped and peeled tomatoes
100 ml red wine
salt and freshly ground black pepper to taste
30 ml (2 Tbsp) chopped fresh coriander
8 sheets phyllo pastry
a little melted butter

1. Place the brinjal in a colander and sprinkle with salt. Allow to stand for 30 minutes before rinsing. Dry well with paper towel.
2. Heat the oil in a large saucepan and fry the onion and garlic.
3. Add the mince and cook until nicely browned.
4. Add the spices, tomato paste, tomatoes and wine. Bring to the boil and add the diced brinjal.
5. Reduce the heat and simmer for 30 minutes until the mince is cooked and the liquid has reduced and thickened. Season to taste.
6. While the mince is simmering, preheat the oven to 200 °C.
7. Spoon the mixture into a two-litre ovenproof casserole dish.
8. Working with one sheet of pastry at a time, brush each sheet with melted butter and, using your fingers, scrunch up and arrange on top of the mince until the surface is completely covered with pastry.
9. Bake for 15–20 minutes or until the pastry is golden-brown.

SERVES 4

Chilli con carne with nachos

This is a quick alternative to cottage pie; the nachos make a great crunchy topping. You can turn it into a plain savoury mince by excluding the chilli and beans.

30 ml (2 Tbsp) olive oil
1 onion, chopped
2 cloves garlic, crushed
2 carrots, peeled and grated
2 stalks celery, chopped
5 ml (1 tsp) chilli powder
10 ml (2 tsp) ground cumin
5ml (1 tsp) ground cinnamon
500 g beef mince
1 x 410 g can red kidney beans, drained and rinsed
1 x 410 g can chopped and peeled tomatoes
30 ml (2 Tbsp) tomato paste
250 ml (1 cup) beef stock
salt and freshly ground black pepper to taste
a handful of chopped fresh coriander
100 g nachos chips
125 ml (½ cup) grated Cheddar cheese
125 ml (½ cup) grated mozzarella cheese

1. Heat the oil and fry the onion, garlic, carrots and celery until soft. Add the spices and cook for 1 minute.
2. Add the mince and cook, breaking up the lumps, until lightly browned.
3. Add the beans, tomatoes, tomato paste and stock, and simmer for 30 minutes. Season well and add the coriander (but reserve a few sprigs as garnish).
4. Preheat the oven to grill.
5. Spoon into a serving dish and arrange a layer of nachos over the top. Top with the cheeses and brown under the grill. Garnish and serve immediately.

SERVES 4

Roast beef with stroganoff sauce

30 ml (2 Tbsp) olive oil
15 ml (1 Tbsp) chopped fresh thyme leaves
5 ml (1 tsp) crushed garlic
salt and freshly ground black pepper to taste
1 kg whole fillet, rump or sirloin
15 ml (1 Tbsp) tomato paste
15 ml (1 Tbsp) Worcestershire sauce
80 ml beef stock
200 g button mushrooms, sliced
1 small onion, thinly sliced
125 ml (½ cup) crème fraîche
15 ml (1 Tbsp) sherry
a few sprigs of fresh thyme

1. Preheat the oven to 200 °C.
2. Combine the oil, chopped thyme, garlic, salt and pepper in a pestle and mortar, and pound lightly until well mixed. Rub all over the surface of the meat.
3. Place the meat in a roasting pan and roast for 20–30 minutes, depending on the cut of meat.
4. Combine the tomato paste, Worcestershire sauce, stock, mushrooms and onion.
5. Remove the meat from the oven and pour over the mushroom sauce. Return to the oven for a further 15–20 minutes for rare to medium, or longer, depending on how you like your meat.
6. When done, transfer the meat from the pan to a plate or board, cover and allow to rest for 10 minutes before carving.
7. In the meantime, add the crème fraîche and sherry to the mushrooms and onions in the pan. Stir until well combined. Spoon this creamy sauce over the sliced meat, garnish with thyme and serve with mashed potato or rice and a vegetable of your choice.

SERVES 4

Sweet and sour beef casserole

125 ml (½ cup) cake flour
salt and pepper to taste
1 kg chuck steak or other stewing beef
1 onion, sliced
1 green pepper, deseeded and sliced
1 x 440 g can pineapple pieces, drained and juice reserved
125 ml (½ cup) beef stock
1 x 400 g can tomato soup
30 ml (2 Tbsp) Worcestershire sauce
4–5 large potatoes, peeled and sliced
a little butter

1. Preheat the oven to 200 °C.
2. Season the flour with salt and pepper and place in a shallow bowl.
3. Cut the meat into bite-sized pieces and toss in the flour.
4. Place the meat in a large casserole dish, shaking off the excess flour. Top with the onion, green pepper and pineapple pieces.
5. Combine the reserved pineapple juice, beef stock, tomato soup and Worcestershire sauce in a jug and pour over the meat.
6. Top with closely overlapping potato slices, brush with a little butter and cover with foil. Cook for 1 hour, then remove the foil and cook for a further 30 minutes or until the potatoes are golden.

SERVES 4

Rustic meatloaf

4 pork sausages
1 red onion, finely chopped
500 g beef mince
30 ml (2 Tbsp) chopped fresh parsley
45 ml (3 Tbsp) tomato pesto
salt and freshly ground black pepper to taste
1 egg, lightly beaten
1 x 410 g can chopped Italian tomatoes
30 ml (2 Tbsp) sweet chilli sauce
30 ml (2 Tbsp) chopped fresh basil

1. Preheat the oven to 180 °C.
2. Slit the sausages down one side and remove the sausage meat. Combine the sausage meat, onion, mince, parsley, pesto, salt, pepper and egg in a bowl. Mix well.
3. Line a baking tray with foil and oil lightly.
4. Shape the mixture into a free-standing meat loaf and place on the baking tray. Gather up the sides of the foil to form a dish.
5. Combine the tomatoes, sweet chilli sauce and basil, and pour over the meat.
6. Bake for 50–60 minutes or until the beef is cooked. Serve with mashed or baked potatoes and seasonal vegetables.

SERVES 4

pork

Stir-fry pork with Asian greens

It's the Chinese 5-spice powder that gives this dish its unusual flavour.

400 g pork fillet
7.5 ml (½ Tbsp) Chinese 5-spice powder
10 ml (2 tsp) chopped fresh garlic
10 ml (2 tsp) grated fresh ginger
30 ml (2 Tbsp) peanut oil
1 red onion, cut into wedges
1 bunch bok choy
1 bunch baby spinach
45 ml (3 Tbsp) oyster sauce
45 ml (3 Tbsp) soy sauce
10 ml (2 tsp) sesame oil
15 ml (1 Tbsp) honey
10 ml (2 tsp) cornflour mixed with water
a few sprigs of fresh coriander to garnish (optional)

1. Cut the pork into slices and then cut each slice in half. Combine with the 5-spice powder, garlic and ginger.
2. Heat the peanut oil in a wok and fry the pork in batches until browned. Remove the meat and set aside.
3. Add a little more oil to the wok and fry the onion until soft. Add the bok choy and spinach, and fry until limp. Return the pork to the wok.
4. Combine the oyster sauce, soy sauce, sesame oil and honey and add to the wok. Bring to the boil, add the cornflour and boil until thickened. Garnish with the coriander (if using) and serve over rice or noodles.

SERVES 4

Cider pork with apple mash

30 ml (2 Tbsp) chopped fresh thyme
30 ml (2 Tbsp) cornflour
1 egg white, lightly beaten with a fork
salt and freshly ground black pepper to taste
600 g spare rib chops or pork fillet, cubed
30 ml (2 Tbsp) olive oil
60 g butter
4 spring onions, finely chopped
250 ml (1 cup) apple cider
125 ml (½ cup) chicken stock
150 ml cream
750 g potatoes, peeled and quartered
1 Granny Smith apple, peeled, cored and quartered
a few spring onions to garnish (optional)

1. Combine the thyme, cornflour, egg white, salt and pepper to make a paste and add the pork pieces. Mix well to coat.
2. Heat the oil and 30 g of the butter in a saucepan and fry the pork over a medium heat until nicely browned. Remove the pork from the pan and set aside.
3. Add the spring onions to the pan and cook for a few minutes before pouring in the cider. Bring to the boil, scraping off any sediment on the base of the pan.
4. Return the pork to the pan and add the stock. Bring to the boil, reduce the heat and simmer for 20–30 minutes or until the pork is cooked and the sauce has reduced. While the pork is cooking, make the apple mash (see step 6).
5. Stir 120 ml cream into the sauce and bring back to the boil. Remove from the heat and serve over apple mash.
6. To make the apple mash, cook the potatoes and apple in boiling salted water for 20–25 minutes until soft. Drain and mash well with the remaining butter and cream. Season well, serve with the cider pork and garnish with a few spring onions, if you like.

SERVES 4

Pork fillet with ponzu

Ponzu is a citrus-flavoured soy sauce that adds a zing to this dish. If you can't find ponzu sauce then use soy sauce with a little lemon rind and juice added to it. Coating the meat in an egg white and cornflour mixture is called velveting. It keeps the meat juicy and tender while cooking.

500 g pork fillet, sliced
1 egg white
15 ml (1 Tbsp) cornflour
15 ml (1 Tbsp) soy sauce
5 ml (1 tsp) chopped fresh garlic
5 ml (1 tsp) grated fresh ginger
30 ml (2 Tbsp) peanut oil
1 red onion, cut into wedges
½ red pepper, deseeded and sliced
½ yellow pepper, deseeded and sliced
1 large carrot, peeled and julienned
60 ml (¼ cup) ponzu sauce
30 ml (2 Tbsp) sweet chilli sauce
15 ml (1 Tbsp) honey

1. Combine the pork, egg white, cornflour, soy sauce, garlic and ginger, and mix well.
2. Heat the oil in a wok or frying pan and fry the pork in two batches so as not to overcrowd the pan. Remove the pork and add the onion, peppers and carrot, and fry for a few minutes.
3. Combine the ponzu sauce, sweet chilli sauce and honey.
4. Return the pork to the pan and add the sauce mixture. Bring to the boil and simmer for 2–3 minutes until the sauce has thickened.
5. Garnish with the coriander (if using) and serve with rice or noodles.

SERVES 4

Caramelised pork and butternut stir-fry

45 ml (3 Tbsp) cooking oil
500 g pork fillet, sliced
250 g butternut, peeled and cut into 1 cm pieces
1 onion, finely chopped
10 ml (2 tsp) crushed garlic
5 ml (1 tsp) crushed fresh ginger
80 ml (1/3 cup) soft brown sugar
60 ml (1/4 cup) fish sauce
60 ml (1/4 cup) rice vinegar
125 ml (1/2 cup) water
45 ml (3 Tbsp) chopped fresh coriander leaves
600 g baby spinach leaves, washed and stalks removed
1 x 175 g punnet snow peas or mangetout

1. Heat 15 ml (1 Tbsp) of the oil in a wok and cook the pork in batches until nicely browned. Remove the pork and set aside.
2. Add the remaining oil to the wok and add the butternut, onion, garlic and ginger. Cook until the butternut is tender but still firm. Remove from the wok and set aside with the pork.
3. Combine the sugar, fish sauce, vinegar and water and add to the wok. Bring to the boil and simmer for 10 minutes or until syrupy.
4. Return the pork and butternut mixture to the wok along with the coriander, spinach and peas. Cook for a few minutes until the spinach has wilted and the peas are cooked. Serve with basmati rice.

SERVES 4

Sweet and sour pork

This colourful dish is better than any Chinese take-away version.

30 ml (2 Tbsp) cooking oil
500 g pork fillet, sliced
1 red onion, cut into wedges
1 red pepper, deseeded and cut into chunks
10 ml (2 tsp) chopped fresh garlic
15 ml (1 Tbsp) chopped fresh ginger
1 x 400 g can pineapple chunks, drained and juice reserved
125 ml (½ cup) water
15 ml (1 Tbsp) soy sauce
60 ml (¼ cup) brown sugar
45 ml (3 Tbsp) cider vinegar
60 ml (¼ cup) tomato sauce
15 ml (1 Tbsp) cornflour
30 ml (2 Tbsp) water
fresh coriander to garnish (optional)

1. Heat the oil in a wok and fry the pork until browned. Remove the pork and set aside.
2. Add the onion, pepper, garlic and ginger to the wok and cook until soft.
3. Add the pineapple chunks and cook for 5 minutes.
4. Combine the reserved pineapple juice, water, soy sauce, sugar, vinegar and tomato sauce, and add to the wok. Return the pork and simmer until cooked through.
5. Combine the cornflour and water and add to the wok. Boil until the sauce thickens. If you like, garnish with the coriander and serve with rice.

SERVES 4

Creamy pan-fried pork

60 ml (¼ cup) cake flour
5 ml (1 tsp) dried sage
salt and freshly ground black pepper to taste
4 pork steaks
45 ml (3 Tbsp) oil
15 ml (1 Tbsp) butter
4 spring onions, white part only, chopped
250 g button mushrooms, sliced
50 ml sherry
250 ml (1 cup) sour cream
15 ml (1 Tbsp) chopped spring onion, green part

1. Place the pork between two sheets of clingfilm and bash with a rolling pin until thin.
2. Combine the flour, sage, salt and pepper and use to coat the pork on both sides.
3. Heat 30 ml (2 Tbsp) of the oil in a frying pan and fry the pork until nicely browned on both sides. Remove from the pan and keep warm.
4. Add the remaining oil and the butter and fry the spring onions (white pieces) for 1 minute. Add the mushrooms and cook for 2–3 minutes before adding the sherry. Stir well, scraping any bits off the base of the frying pan.
5. Stir in the sour cream and return the pork to the pan. Cook for a further 5–8 minutes. Sprinkle with the green spring onion pieces and serve with rice noodles on the side.

SERVES 4

Ten-minute chops with orange glaze

30 ml (2 Tbsp) olive oil
4 smoked kassler chops

ORANGE GLAZE
3–4 oranges
a little water
45 ml (3 Tbsp) honey
30 ml (2 Tbsp) soft brown sugar
5 ml (1 tsp) soy sauce
5 ml (1 tsp) wholegrain mustard

1. Heat the oil in a saucepan and fry the chops for 4–5 minutes on each side until cooked through. Set aside the pan.
2. To make the glaze, remove the rind from one of the oranges using a zester. Place in a saucepan with a little water and boil for 5 minutes. Strain, reserving the rind.
3. Squeeze 250 ml (1 cup) juice from the oranges and combine with the honey, sugar, soy sauce and mustard in the saucepan. Bring to the boil and then simmer for 5 minutes. Add the rind and remove from the heat.
4. Pour the glaze over the chops in the saucepan and reheat. Serve immediately with a green salad.

SERVES 4

Barbecue rib chops

60 ml (¼ cup) hoisin sauce
15 ml (1 Tbsp) sherry
60 ml (¼ cup) soy sauce
10 ml (2 tsp) chopped fresh garlic
10 ml (2 tsp) grated fresh ginger
15 ml (1 Tbsp) chopped fresh coriander
45 ml (3 Tbsp) olive oil
4 pork spare rib chops

1. Combine the hoisin sauce, sherry, soy sauce, garlic, ginger, coriander and 15 ml (1 Tbsp) of the oil in a Pyrex dish.
2. Add the pork chops and turn to coat with the sauce. Allow to stand for 15–20 minutes.
3. Brush a heavy-based grill pan with a little oil and heat over medium heat.
4. Remove the pork chops from the marinade and cook for 8–10 minutes on each side or until cooked through. Baste during cooking. Alternatively, these can be cooked under a preheated oven grill.
5. Serve with chips and a salad.

SERVES 4

Slow-cooker pulled pork

My sister, who lives in America, introduced me to this dish. It does take a long time to cook, but is no trouble at all to make. Put it on in the morning and when you come home from work your house will smell delicious and you will have a warm meal ready for the family – Jenny.

1.5 kg pork neck
2 large onions, sliced
125 ml (½ cup) tomato sauce
80 ml (⅓ cup) cider vinegar
80 ml (⅓ cup) brown sugar
60 ml (¼ cup) tomato paste
45 ml (3 Tbsp) Worcestershire sauce
30 ml (2 Tbsp) paprika
5 ml (1 tsp) salt
water, enough to cover

1. Put the pork into the slow cooker and layer the onion slices on top.
2. Combine the remaining ingredients and mix well. Pour over the pork and then add enough water to cover. Switch the slow cooker on to high and leave for 8–10 hours.
3. Carefully remove the meat from the slow cooker and use two forks to pull the pork apart.
4. Put about 500 ml (2 cups) of the sauce from the cooker into a saucepan and simmer on the stove for 10 minutes until reduced and slightly thickened. Pour enough sauce over the pork to moisten it.
5. Serve the pulled pork on soft rolls, wrapped in tortillas or on sandwiches. It is traditionally served with gherkins and coleslaw.

Note: For an even quicker option, instead of making the sauce you can use a 750 ml bottle of your favourite barbecue sauce.

SERVES 6–8

Pork steaks with apples

Pork, apples and sage are a classic combination. Use tart green apples that can hold up to cooking without disintegrating.

15 ml (1 Tbsp) olive oil
4 pork steaks
salt and freshly ground black pepper to taste
2 onions, halved and sliced
2 apples, peeled, cored and cut into wedges
15 ml (1 Tbsp) sugar
a handful of fresh sage leaves
3–4 juniper berries, crushed (optional)
1 x 340 ml bottle cider or apple juice

1. Heat the oil in a frying pan and fry the steaks until browned on both sides. Season with salt and pepper. Remove the pork from the pan and set aside.
2. Add the onions and apples to the pan and cook until the onions are soft.
3. Add the sugar and cook for a few minutes. Add the sage, juniper berries and cider. Return the pork to the pan, cover and simmer until the steaks are cooked through and the sauce has reduced. Serve with creamy mashed potatoes.

SERVES 4

lamb

Quick lamb in pitas

60 ml (¼ cup) olive oil
10 ml (2 tsp) chopped fresh garlic
5 ml (1 tsp) grated lemon rind
45 ml (3 Tbsp) lemon juice
15 ml (1 Tbsp) chopped fresh origanum
15 ml (1 Tbsp) chopped fresh thyme leaves
500 g lamb steaks, cut into strips
salt and black pepper to taste
4 pita breads
60 ml (¼ cup) Greek yoghurt
60 ml (¼ cup) crumbled feta cheese

1. Combine the olive oil, garlic, lemon rind, lemon juice and herbs.
2. Add the lamb, mix well and set aside for 30 minutes.
3. Heat a non-stick frying pan and fry the lamb strips in batches over a high heat until just done; the lamb should still be slightly pink. Season well and remove from the heat.
4. Warm the pita breads and split open. Pile the meat into the pita, top each with a spoonful of Greek yoghurt and sprinkle over the feta cheese and any leftover fresh herbs.

SERVES 4

Lamb burgers with tahini sauce

Instead of serving burger patties on buns, which I often find too much too eat, a piece of toasted ciabatta bread works just as well and is delicious. The choice is yours. When you make your own patties you can shape them to fit a panini or a slice of bread. These burgers are delicious made with ostrich mince as well.

olive oil
6 slices ciabatta bread, toasted
fresh salad leaves (e.g. rocket or baby spinach)
2–3 tomatoes, sliced
1 red onion, thinly sliced

BURGERS
500 g lamb mince
2 slices bread, crumbed
1 red onion, roughly chopped
10 ml (2 tsp) chopped fresh garlic
5 ml (1 tsp) ground coriander
5 ml (1 tsp) ground cumin
5 ml (1 tsp) salt
30 ml (2 Tbsp) sweet chilli sauce
1 egg
45 ml (3 Tbsp) chopped fresh coriander

TAHINI SAUCE
60 ml (¼ cup) Greek yoghurt
30 ml (2 Tbsp) tahini
15 ml (1 Tbsp) honey

1. Put all the ingredients for the burgers into a food processor and process until well mixed. Divide the mixture into six portions and shape into patties. Brush the patties with olive oil and cook on a griddle pan.
2. To make the tahini sauce, combine all the ingredients and mix well.
3. Top the toasted ciabatta slices with the salad leaves. Position a burger patty on top of each slice, add a spoonful of tahini sauce, followed by sliced tomato and sliced onion.

MAKES 6 BURGERS

Lamb and barley soup

45 ml (3 Tbsp) olive oil
500 g neck of lamb
1 onion, chopped
3–4 leeks, sliced
10–15 ml (2–3 tsp) paprika
3 carrots, peeled and diced
2–3 stalks celery, chopped
2 potatoes, peeled and diced
2 litres (8 cups) water
250 ml (1 cup) pearl barley
salt and freshly ground black pepper to taste

1. Heat the oil in a large saucepan and fry the lamb in batches until browned. Remove from the pan and set aside.
2. Add the onion and leeks to the saucepan and cook until soft. Add the paprika and cook for 1 minute.
3. Add the carrots, celery and potatoes and cook for 2–3 minutes.
4. Add the water and barley, return the lamb to the pan and simmer, partially covered, for 1–1½ hours until the meat is very soft.
5. Remove the lamb from the pan and cut into pieces, discarding any bones. Return to the soup and season well with salt and pepper before serving.

SERVES 6–8

Aromatic lamb with chickpeas

60 ml (¼ cup) olive oil
10 ml (2 tsp) ground cumin
5 ml (1 tsp) ground cinnamon
5 ml (1 tsp) ground ginger
5 ml (1 tsp) turmeric
25 ml (5 tsp) hot water
salt and freshly ground black pepper to taste
1 kg leg of lamb, cubed
2 onions, chopped
5 ml (1 tsp) crushed garlic
1 x 410 g can whole peeled tomatoes
250 ml (1 cup) chicken stock
1 x 400 g can chickpeas, well drained
rind of 1 lemon
rind and juice of 1 orange
a little sugar if necessary
a handful of fresh coriander, chopped

1. In a large bowl, combine half of the olive oil with the cumin, cinnamon, ginger, turmeric, hot water, salt and pepper. Add the cubed lamb, toss well in the spice mixture and set aside for at least 20 minutes.
2. Heat the remaining oil in a heavy-based pan and fry the lamb in batches until well browned. Remove the meat from the pan and set aside.
3. Add the onions to the pan and fry until soft. Stir in the garlic and tomatoes.
4. Return the lamb to the pan and add the stock. Reduce the heat and simmer for about 1½ hours or until the meat is tender.
5. Stir in the chickpeas, lemon rind, orange rind and orange juice. Season to taste and add a little sugar if necessary. Simmer, uncovered, for a further 20–30 minutes. Serve garnished with coriander over basmati rice.

SERVES 6

Lamb curry in a hurry

By using a tender cut of meat, this curry can be ready in less than 30 minutes. It also tastes great made with korma curry paste.

15 ml (1 Tbsp) olive oil
800 g lamb steaks, cubed
1 red onion, cut into thin wedges
1 red pepper, deseeded and diced
45 ml (3 Tbsp) tikka masala curry paste
1 x 410 g can chopped and peeled tomatoes
250 ml (1 cup) coconut milk
200 g baby spinach leaves
salt and freshly ground black pepper to taste
60 ml (¼ cup) chopped fresh coriander

1. Heat the oil in a saucepan and fry the lamb in batches until browned, but not cooked through. Remove from the pan and set aside.
2. Add the onion and pepper to the pan and fry until the onion is soft. Stir in the curry paste and cook for 1 minute.
3. Add the tomatoes and coconut milk and simmer until the sauce is thickened.
4. Return the meat to the pan along with the spinach and cook for 5–8 minutes until the spinach is wilted and the meat is cooked.
5. Season to taste and add the coriander before serving with basmati rice.

SERVES 4

Spicy lamb with yoghurt

5 ml (1 tsp) sea salt
10–15 ml (2–3 tsp) curry power
125 ml (½ cup) Greek yoghurt
12 lamb loin chops
30 ml (2 Tbsp) olive oil
2 onions, sliced
10 ml (2 tsp) grated fresh ginger
10 ml (2 tsp) crushed garlic
1 stick cinnamon
1 tomato, chopped
375 ml (1½ cups) vegetable stock
15 ml (1 Tbsp) tomato paste
30 ml (2 Tbsp) chopped fresh coriander

1. Add the sea salt and 5 ml (1 tsp) of the curry powder to the yoghurt. Coat the chops with this mixture and set aside.
2. Heat the oil in a saucepan and fry the onions slowly for about 10 minutes until soft and light golden-brown.
3. Add the remaining curry powder and fry for a few seconds, and then add the ginger, garlic, cinnamon stick and tomato.
4. Add the chops and yoghurt and cook for a few more minutes.
5. Combine the stock and tomato paste and pour over the chops. Bring to the boil, reduce the heat and simmer, uncovered, for 20–30 minutes or until the lamb is tender and the sauce has thickened.
6. Sprinkle over the fresh coriander and serve with basmati rice.

SERVES 4–6

Lamb chops 3 ways

Lemon and herb lamb chops

15 ml (1 Tbsp) olive oil
10 ml (2 tsp) crushed garlic
30 ml (2 Tbsp) lemon juice
30 ml (2 Tbsp) chopped fresh origanum
15 ml (1 Tbsp) chopped fresh mint
15 ml (1 Tbsp) chopped fresh parsley
salt and freshly ground black pepper to taste
4–8 lamb chops, depending on their size

1. Combine the olive oil, garlic, lemon juice, herbs and seasoning.
2. Place the chops in a dish, pour over the mixture and set aside for 30 minutes.
3. Cook the chops on a griddle pan or under a heated grill until done to your liking. Serve immediately.

SERVES 4

Dukkah lamb chops

4–8 lamb chops, depending on their size
30 ml (2 Tbsp) olive oil
salt and freshly ground black pepper to taste
50 ml dukkah of your choice

1. Brush the chops with the olive oil and season with salt and pepper.
2. Cook on a griddle pan or under the grill until done to your liking.
3. Remove and dip each chop into the dukkah until well coated. Serve immediately.

Note: It is better to coat the meat with dukkah after cooking, as the dukkah tends to burn if you coat the chops with it beforehand.

SERVES 4

Cumin-spiced lamb chops

5 ml (1 tsp) ground cumin
salt and freshly ground black pepper to taste
30 ml (2 Tbsp) olive oil
15 ml (1 Tbsp) lemon juice
15 ml (1 Tbsp) chopped fresh rosemary
4–8 lamb chops, depending on their size

1. Combine the cumin, salt, pepper, oil, lemon juice and rosemary.
2. Rub the mixture into the chops and set aside for 30 minutes.
3. Cook the chops on a griddle pan or under a heated grill until done to your liking. Serve immediately.

SERVES 4

Lemon and herb lamb chops

Lamb casserole

8 lamb neck chops
60 ml (¼ cup) seasoned flour
30 ml (2 Tbsp) olive oil
1 kg potatoes, thickly sliced
3 carrots, peeled and sliced
3 onions, sliced into thick rounds
a few sprigs of fresh thyme or lemon thyme
salt and freshly ground black pepper to taste
125 g streaky bacon, chopped and fried
15 ml (1 Tbsp) tomato paste
500 ml (2 cups) beef stock

1. Coat the chops in the seasoned flour.
2. Heat the oil in a large heavy-based saucepan and brown the chops on both sides over a high heat. Set aside,
3. Preheat the oven to 180 °C.
4. Arrange half of the potato slices, carrots, onions and thyme in a deep, heavy-based ovenproof dish. Season to taste and add half of the bacon.
5. Layer the chops on top and cover with the remaining potato slices, carrots, onions, bacon and thyme.
6. Mix the tomato paste and stock together and pour into the dish.
7. Cover and cook for 2–2½ hours or until the potatoes and chops are soft.

SERVES 4–6

Citrus lamb with sweet potato and coriander

600 g leg of lamb or lamb steaks, cut into small cubes
15 ml (1 Tbsp) Moroccan spice rub or Moroccan lamb spice
15 ml (1 Tbsp) cake flour
30 ml (2 Tbsp) olive oil
500 g sweet potato or celeriac, peeled and cut into 5mm slices
1 lemon, sliced
1 orange, sliced
1 onion, chopped
15 ml (1 Tbsp), grated fresh ginger
30 ml (2 Tbsp) honey
2 bay leaves
375 ml (1½ cups) chicken or vegetable stock
60 ml (¼ cup) chopped coriander
30 ml (2 Tbsp) sour cream or crème fraîche

1. Place the lamb in a mixing bowl and sprinkle over the spice and flour. Toss well to coat.
2. Heat half the oil in a saucepan and fry the sweet potato or celeriac for about 5 minutes. Add the lemon and orange slices, reserving a few for garnish, and cook for a further few minutes. Remove from the saucepan and set aside.
3. Add a little more oil to the saucepan and fry the onion and ginger until softened and then add the lamb and fry until nicely browned.
4. Reduce heat to low. Stir in the honey and cook for a few minutes, mixing well.
5. Add the bay leaves and stock. Season with salt and pepper, cover and simmer for 30 minutes.
6. Remove from the heat and stir in the sweet potato/celeriac mixture. Return to the heat, cover and cook for a further 30-40 minutes or until the lamb and sweet potato are cooked. Add extra stock if needed.
7. Stir in the chopped coriander and the sour cream or crème fraîche just before serving.

SERVES 4

fish

Trout tabbouleh

This dish is great to make in summer, as the taste of lemon is very refreshing. You can replace the trout with canned flaked pink salmon.

250 ml (1 cup) water
150 ml white wine
½ onion, sliced
2 slices of lemon
2 bay leaves
500–600 g lightly smoked trout fillet
350 g bulgur wheat or cooked pearl barley
1 red onion, chopped
1 small cucumber, diced
1 red pepper, deseeded and diced
1 yellow pepper, deseeded and diced
60 ml (¼ cup) chopped fresh parsley
30 ml (2 Tbsp) chopped fresh mint
125 ml (½ cup) olive oil
80 ml (⅓ cup) lime or lemon juice
1 clove garlic, crushed
salt and freshly ground black pepper to taste

1. In a large pan, bring the water, wine, onion, lemon slices and bay leaves to a simmer.
2. Add the trout and poach gently for 5–10 minutes until just cooked. Remove from the pan and drain. When cool, flake into bite-size pieces.
3. Pour cold water over the bulgur wheat and soak for 10 minutes. Set aside in a sieve until well drained and dry. (If using cooked pearl barley, omit this step.)
4. Place the bulgur wheat or pearl barley in a bowl and add the red onion, cucumber, peppers, parsley and mint.
5. Combine the oil, lime or lemon juice and garlic. Pour over the bulgur or barley mixture and mix well. Season to taste.
6. Carefully mix in the trout, taking care not to break up the fish too much.

SERVES 4

Fish laksa

The sweet, sour, salty and spicy flavours of this soup are addictive. Save time by buying a packet of udon noodles that are already cooked.

125 g egg or rice noodles
1 x 400 g can coconut milk
80 g laksa paste
500 ml (2 cups) fish stock
600 g frozen hake medallions
50 ml lime juice
15–20 ml (3–4 tsp) fish sauce
125 ml (½ cup) chopped fresh coriander or sliced green pepper

1. Place the egg or rice noodles in a bowl and cover with boiling water. Set aside for 10–15 minutes until the noodles are soft.
2. Heat the coconut milk and laksa paste in a wok, stirring until the mixture begins to boil.
3. Add the stock and simmer for 5 minutes.
4. Cut each piece of fish into four pieces and add to the wok. Simmer gently for 3–5 minutes until the fish is cooked.
5. Drain the noodles and add to the wok. Stir in the lime juice, fish sauce and coriander or green pepper slices, and serve immediately.

SERVES 4

Lemon and herb fish parcels

This dish is a favourite as there are no pots and pans to wash up after cooking.

120 g spinach leaves
4 fish fillets
1 small red pepper, deseeded and sliced
1 small yellow pepper, deseeded and sliced
1 red onion, thinly sliced
20 black olives, pitted
1 red chilli, deseeded and chopped
80 ml (⅓ cup) olive oil
30 ml (2 Tbsp) lemon juice
5 ml (1 tsp) grated lemon rind
5 ml (1 tsp) chopped fresh garlic
30 ml (2 Tbsp) chopped fresh mint
30 ml (2 Tbsp) chopped fresh basil
a handful of fresh chives, snipped

1. Preheat the oven to 190 °C.
2. Cut four 30 cm square sheets of foil and lay on the work surface. Cut four sheets of baking paper the same size and lay them on top of the foil.
3. Divide the spinach leaves between the parcels and place a fish fillet on top of each.
4. Divide the peppers, onion, olives and chilli between the parcels and scatter over the fish.
5. Combine the olive oil, lemon juice, lemon rind, garlic and herbs, and divide this mixture between the parcels.
6. Wrap up each parcel and bake for 10–15 minutes until the fish is cooked.

MAKES 4 PARCELS

Red fish curry

Frozen hake medallions don't break up too quickly when cooked from frozen. If you use fresh fish make sure it's a firm one to prevent it from breaking up too much.

15 ml (1 Tbsp) sunflower oil
1 red onion, thinly sliced
10–15 ml (2–3 tsp) red curry paste
1 x 400 g can coconut milk
120 g baby button mushrooms
125 g fine green beans, cut into 2 cm pieces
500 g frozen hake medallions
15 ml (1 Tbsp) lime juice
20–25 ml (4–5 tsp) fish sauce
10 ml (2 tsp) brown sugar
1 red chilli, deseeded and thinly sliced
60 ml (¼ cup) chopped fresh coriander
60 ml (¼ cup) chopped fresh basil

1. Heat the oil in a wok and gently fry the onion until soft. Add the curry paste and cook for a few minutes until fragrant. Take care not to have the heat too high or the paste will burn.
2. Add the coconut milk and simmer for 2 minutes, then add the mushrooms and beans and simmer until the liquid has reduced slightly.
3. Add the fish and gently simmer until just cooked. Do not stir too much as this will break up the fish.
4. Add the lime juice, fish sauce and sugar.
5. Remove from the heat and stir in the chilli, coriander and basil before serving with jasmine rice.

SERVES 4

Lemon and herb fish parcels

Spicy-topped fish

4 thick hake filets, about 100 g each
10 ml (2 tsp) sea salt
1 onion, roughly chopped
5 ml (1 tsp) chopped fresh garlic
5 ml (1 tsp) grated fresh ginger
30 ml (2 Tbsp) Greek yoghurt
30 ml (2 Tbsp) curry paste
15 ml (1 Tbsp) chutney
125 ml (½ cup) fresh breadcrumbs
30 ml (2 Tbsp) chopped fresh coriander
salt and freshly ground black pepper to taste

1. Preheat the oven to 180 °C. Line a baking tray with foil and lightly grease with butter.
2. Sprinkle the fish fillets with a little sea salt and set aside.
3. Combine the onion, garlic and ginger in a food processor and process until finely chopped. Add the yoghurt, curry paste and chutney and blend to a thick paste. Add the breadcrumbs, coriander, salt and pepper, and mix well.
4. Place the fish fillets on the baking tray and spread the paste evenly over them. Bake for 12–15 minutes or until the fish is cooked through. Serve with vegetables or a salad of your choice.

SERVES 4

Herb-crusted fish fillets

Use either white or brown bread for the crumbs. This crumb mixture also works well on flattened chicken breast fillets.

4 white fish fillets (such as hake)
salt and freshly ground black pepper to taste
3 slices bread, crumbed
45 ml (3 Tbsp) chopped fresh herbs
80 ml (⅓ cup) grated Parmesan cheese
250 ml (1 cup) cake flour
2 eggs, beaten
a little olive oil

1. Sprinkle the fish with salt.
2. Combine the breadcrumbs, herbs and Parmesan cheese in a bowl, and season with salt and pepper.
3. Put the flour and beaten egg into separate bowls.
4. Dip the fish fillets one at a time in the flour, then in the egg and finally in the breadcrumbs.
5. Heat a little oil in a non-stick frying pan and fry the fish for about 4 minutes a side until golden-brown on both sides. Drain on paper towel and serve with a side salad and potato wedges.

SERVES 4

A trio of salmon

Chilli and lime salmon trout

This sweet, sour and spicy sauce goes well with salmon. In winter, this dish is great served with wasabi mashed potatoes.

4 salmon trout fillets
salt and freshly ground black pepper to taste
15 ml (1 Tbsp) olive oil
125 ml (½ cup) sweet chilli sauce
30 ml (2 Tbsp) fish sauce
60 ml (¼ cup) lime juice
30 ml (2 Tbsp) honey
rocket leaves
1 red chilli, deseeded and sliced

1. Season the fish with the salt and pepper.
2. Heat the oil in a frying pan and fry the fillets to the desired doneness. Remove from pan and keep warm.
3. Combine the sweet chilli sauce, fish sauce, lime juice and honey, and add to the pan. Bring to the boil and remove from the heat.
4. Serve each salmon fillet on a bed of rocket with the sauce poured over and sprinkled with red chilli.

SERVES 4

Honey-glazed salmon

4 salmon steaks
salt and freshly ground black pepper to taste

MARINADE
45 ml (3 Tbsp) olive oil
45 ml (3 Tbsp) lemon juice
15 ml (1 Tbsp) honey
30 ml (2 Tbsp) tomato pesto
15 ml (1 Tbsp) chopped fresh basil
5 ml (1 tsp) crushed garlic

1. Combine the marinade ingredients in a small jug and mix well.
2. Put the fish in an ovenproof dish and pour over the marinade. Cover and allow to stand for 30 minutes.
3. Preheat the oven to 200 °C. Line a baking tray with foil and grease.
4. When ready to cook, transfer the fish to the baking tray, season with the salt and pepper and cook for 6 minutes on each side. Brush with the marinade occasionally while cooking.
5. Serve with mash and steamed vegetables.

SERVES 4

Pesto-crusted salmon

butter for greasing
4 salmon steaks
5 ml (1 tsp) sea salt
freshly ground black pepper to taste
1 lemon
125 ml (½ cup) basil pesto
375 ml (1½ cups) fresh breadcrumbs

1. Line a baking tray with foil and grease with a little butter.
2. Place the salmon steaks, skin side down, on the baking tray and season with the salt and pepper and a squeeze of lemon juice. Cover and allow to rest for 15 minutes.
3. Preheat the oven to 200 °C.
4. Combine the pesto and breadcrumbs in a small bowl. Divide the mixture into four and press evenly into the top of each salmon steak.
5. Bake for 12–15 minutes or until the salmon is cooked to your liking.
6. Serve with mashed potatoes and seasonal vegetables.

SERVES 4

pizza & pasta

Pasta with chorizo

Adding sliced avocado just before serving really makes this dish pop!

30 ml (2 Tbsp) olive oil
3–4 chorizo sausages, sliced
1 red onion, halved and cut into thin wedges
10 ml (2 tsp) chopped fresh garlic
250 g mushrooms, sliced
1 red or green chilli, deseeded and chopped
1 x 400 g can cherry tomatoes
15 ml (1 Tbsp) chopped fresh rosemary
salt and freshly ground black pepper to taste
300 g linguini pasta
125 ml (½ cup) grated Parmesan cheese

1. Heat the oil in a large frying pan and fry the chorizo for 2–3 minutes. Remove from the pan and set aside.
2. Add the onion, garlic, mushrooms and chilli to the pan and cook until the onion is soft.
3. Add the tomatoes, rosemary, salt and pepper and simmer until the sauce is reduced and thickened. Return the chorizo to the pan.
4. Cook the pasta in salted boiling water until *al dente*, drain and add to the sauce.
5. Toss to coat pasta and serve topped with Parmesan cheese.

SERVES 4

Frying pan pizza

Making a yeast dough for pizza can be a little time consuming, so this recipe will save you stacks of time. Leftovers are delicious tucked into lunch boxes.

BASE
500 ml (2 cups) self-raising flour
5 ml (1 tsp) salt
180 ml grated Cheddar cheese
30 ml (2 Tbsp) snipped chives
45 ml (3 Tbsp) olive oil
150–180 ml water

TOPPING
20 ml (4 tsp) olive oil + extra for drizzling
30 ml (2 Tbsp) tomato pesto
250 ml (1 cup) grated mozzarella cheese
your choice of olives, tomatoes, mushrooms, ham, pineapple and red onion
fresh wild rocket or basil leaves
1 avocado, peeled and sliced

1. To make the bases, combine the flour, salt, Cheddar cheese and chives in a mixing bowl. Add the olive oil and enough water to bring the dough together to form a ball that is slightly soft but not sticky.
2. Lightly knead the dough and divide into two pieces. Roll out each piece into a 20 cm disc.
3. In a non-stick frying pan, heat 10 ml (2 tsp) of the olive oil, making sure it is spread over the base of the pan. Add one disc of dough. Put on the lid of the pan and cook for about 5 minutes until the base is golden-brown. Turn over and cook on the other side for about 5 minutes. Place the cooked base on a baking tray. Repeat with the second disc of dough, placing it on the same baking tray as the first.
4. Preheat the oven to grill.
5. Spread the bases with the tomato pesto and sprinkle over the mozzarella cheese. Arrange your desired toppings over the cheese and then place under the grill until the cheese has melted.
6. Remove from the oven and top with a handful of the fresh wild rocket or basil leaves, sliced avocado and a drizzle of olive oil. Serve immediately.

MAKES 2 PIZZAS

Quick pizza

Because you don't need the pizza base to rise to any great height you don't have to wait long for your dough to rise. All you really want from the dough is to have a bread-like taste and texture. Feel free to use ready-prepared bread dough from your local supermarket.

BASE
1 litre (4 cups) cake flour
10 ml (2 tsp) salt
15 ml (1 Tbsp) sugar
10 g instant yeast
30 ml (2 Tbsp) olive oil
400–500 ml warm water

TOPPING
125 ml (½ cup) bottled tomato pasta sauce
250 ml (1 cup) grated mozzarella cheese
your choice of mushrooms, caramelised onions, tomatoes, ham, pineapple, salami, bacon and avocado
salad leaves to garnish

1. To make the bases, combine the flour, salt, sugar and yeast in a bowl. Add the olive oil and enough warm water to make a dough that is soft but not sticky.
2. Knead well until the dough is smooth, and then place in an oiled plastic bag and leave to rise for 15–20 minutes.
3. Preheat the oven to 220 °C.
4. Remove the dough from the bag and knead gently before dividing into four portions. Roll each portion into a disc about the size of a dinner plate (or press into any shaped roasting pan to make individual pizzas).
5. Spread a spoonful of tomato pasta sauce over each base. Top with the mozzarella cheese and your choice of toppings.
6. Bake for 8–10 minutes until the base is golden and the cheese has melted. Garnish with the salad leaves.

MAKES 4 PIZZAS

Broccoli and lemon pasta

This is a great dish to encourage children to eat extra vegetables – if you don't tell them it's made with broccoli, they will never guess.

250 g wholewheat linguini pasta
400 g broccoli, broken into florets
10 ml (2 tsp) chopped fresh garlic
1 red chilli, deseeded and chopped
grated rind of 1 lemon
45 ml (3 Tbsp) lemon juice
250 ml (1 cup) grated Parmesan cheese + extra for serving
80 ml (⅓ cup) olive oil
salt and freshly ground black pepper to taste
50 g toasted pine nuts

1. Boil the pasta in a pot of salted water until *al dente*. Drain, reserving about 125 ml (½ cup) of the cooking liquid.
2. Steam or boil the broccoli until soft. Drain and mash well.
3. Put the broccoli into a deep saucepan and add the garlic, chilli, lemon rind, lemon juice, Parmesan cheese and olive oil. Stir well and heat through.
4. Add the drained pasta along with the reserved cooking liquid, season and toss well to combine.
5. Mix in the pine nuts and serve topped with extra Parmesan cheese.

SERVES 4

Penne with tuna and capers

A store-cupboard staple, tuna goes so well with pasta. Use any shape of pasta to replace penne if you prefer.

300 g penne pasta
15 ml (1 Tbsp) olive oil
1 red onion, sliced into thin wedges
2 cloves garlic, crushed
1 red chilli, deseeded and chopped
4 tomatoes, roughly chopped
1 red pepper, deseeded and diced
45 ml (3 Tbsp) capers, drained and rinsed
a handful of fresh wild rocket
1 x 170 g can tuna in water, drained and flaked
125 ml (½ cup) grated Parmesan cheese
salt and freshly ground black pepper to taste

1. Cook the pasta according to the packet instructions in a large saucepan of salted boiling water.
2. In the meantime, heat the oil in a large frying pan over medium heat and cook the onion, garlic and chilli for 2–3 minutes or until the onion is soft.
3. Increase the heat to high and add the tomatoes, red pepper and capers. Cook, stirring occasionally, for 4–5 minutes or until the vegetables are soft.
4. Drain the pasta, reserving 50–60 ml of the cooking water. Return the pasta and reserved water to the saucepan, add the tomato mixture, rocket, tuna and most of the Parmesan cheese.
5. Season with salt and pepper and toss until combined and heated through. Serve sprinkled with the remaining Parmesan cheese.

SERVES 4

Carbonara with peppers and bacon

Supper in a jiffy.

250 g pasta of your choice (spaghetti is the norm)
30 ml (2 Tbsp) olive oil
250 g diced bacon
2 extra-large eggs
2 egg yolks
125 ml (½ cup) cream
60 g Parmesan cheese, grated
1 onion, chopped
5 ml (1 tsp) crushed garlic
1 green pepper, deseeded and diced
1 red pepper, deseeded and diced
salt and freshly ground black pepper to taste
30 ml (2 Tbsp) chopped fresh flat-leaf parsley

1. Cook the pasta according to the package instructions. Drain and toss with a little olive oil.
2. Heat the 30 ml (2 Tbsp) olive oil in a saucepan and fry the bacon until crispy. Remove the bacon, drain on paper towel and set aside.
3. Combine the eggs, egg yolks, cream and Parmesan cheese in a bowl and set aside.
4. Fry the onion, garlic and peppers in the saucepan that you used to fry the bacon. Add the pasta, remove the pan from the heat and immediately stir in the egg mixture. There should be sufficient heat to just scramble the eggs slightly, but not to overcook or the eggs will curdle.
5. Season to taste, sprinkle over the parsley and serve immediately.

SERVES 4

Pasta with avocado and prosciutto

This dish was born out of raiding the fridge for anything to add to some cooked pasta. The combination works really well, but if you don't have some of the ingredients, use whatever you have.

15 ml (1 Tbsp) olive oil
125 g prosciutto or bacon
125 g cherry tomatoes, halved
1 avocado, peeled and diced
125 g feta cheese, crumbled
a handful of black olives, pitted and halved
300 g pasta of your choice
a handful of fresh basil, torn (optional)
125 ml (½ cup) grated Parmesan cheese
freshly ground black pepper to taste

1. Heat the oil in a large frying pan and fry the prosciutto or bacon until crisp. Remove from the pan, roughly chop and set aside.
2. Add the tomatoes to the pan and cook until slightly softened, then add the avocado, feta cheese and olives and toss to combine.
3. Cook the pasta in a pot of salted water until *al dente*. Drain, reserving some of the cooking liquid.
4. Add the pasta to the pan, along with the chopped prosciutto or bacon and the basil (if using). Add a little reserved cooking liquid and toss to combine everything.
5. Serve topped with grated Parmesan cheese and a grinding of pepper to taste.

SERVES 4

Broccoli and tuna pasta bake

250 g fusilli pasta
250 g broccoli, broken into florets
125 ml (½ cup) frozen peas
30 ml (2 Tbsp) olive oil
1 onion, chopped
2 x 170 g cans tuna in water, drained
2 extra-large eggs
250 ml (1 cup) fresh cream
250 ml (1 cup) grated Cheddar cheese
salt and freshly ground black pepper to taste
80 ml (⅓ cup) grated Parmesan cheese

1. Cook the pasta according to the package instructions. Then, 5 minutes before the end of cooking time, add the broccoli and peas. Cook for the remaining 5 minutes and drain. Return to the saucepan.
2. In the meantime, heat the oil in a saucepan over medium heat and cook the onion until softened. Stir in the tuna and add to the pasta and broccoli.
3. Preheat the oven to 180 °C.
4. Combine the eggs and cream and beat lightly with a fork. Stir into the pasta along with half of the Cheddar cheese. Season to taste.
5. Spoon the mixture into a greased ovenproof dish and sprinkle over the remaining Cheddar cheese as well as the Parmesan cheese. Bake for 20–30 minutes or until golden-brown.

SERVES 4

vegetarian

Lentil cottage pie

You won't even miss the meat in this dish. It also works well using sweet potatoes for the topping. The mixture is delicious on toast or as a filling for baked potatoes.

30 ml (2 Tbsp) olive oil
1 large onion, finely chopped
2–3 stalks celery, chopped
2 large carrots, peeled and grated
10 ml (2 tsp) chopped fresh garlic
250 ml (1 cup) tomato passata
30 ml (2 Tbsp) tomato paste
1 bay leaf
15 ml (1 Tbsp) chopped fresh thyme
250 ml (1 cup) vegetable stock
1 x 400 g can lentils, drained and rinsed
salt and freshly ground black pepper to taste
800 g floury potatoes, peeled and chopped
50 g butter
60–80 ml (¼ – ⅓ cup) milk

1. Heat the oil in a saucepan over medium heat and cook the onion for 5 minutes.
2. Add the celery, carrots and garlic and cook for 2–3 minutes.
3. Add the tomato passata, tomato paste, bay leaf, thyme and stock, and simmer gently for 20–30 minutes until the vegetables are cooked.
4. Stir in the lentils and season well. Remove from the heat.
5. Preheat the oven to 180 °C.
6. To make the potato topping, boil the potatoes in a saucepan of water until soft. Drain and mash with the butter and milk. Season well with salt and pepper.
7. Transfer the lentil mixture to an ovenproof baking dish, top with the mashed potato and bake for 20 minutes.

SERVES 4

Root vegetable soup

250 ml (1 cup) green split peas, soaked overnight
50 g butter
1–2 large leeks, sliced
2 carrots, peeled and chopped
2–3 stalks celery, chopped
3 potatoes, peeled and chopped
2 litres (8 cups) chicken or vegetable stock
salt and freshly ground black pepper to taste
45 ml (3 Tbsp) chopped fresh parsley

1. Drain the split peas and set aside.
2. In a large saucepan, melt the butter and fry the leeks, carrots and celery until slightly softened.
3. Add the potatoes, stock and split peas and simmer, covered, for 30–40 minutes until the vegetables and peas are very soft.
4. Remove from the heat and purée in a food processor or using a hand blender. Season to taste and stir in the parsley. Serve with crusty bread.

Note: Although the split peas do not need to be soaked, you will find that by soaking them they cook more quickly and have a softer texture.

SERVES 6–8

Chickpea fritters

2 x 400 g cans chickpeas, drained and rinsed
3 spring onions, finely chopped
60 ml (¼ cup) plain yoghurt
10–15 ml (2–3 tsp) curry powder
5 ml (1 tsp) ground cumin
5 ml (1 tsp) ground coriander
1 egg
375 ml (1½ cups) fresh breadcrumbs
125 ml (½ cup) chopped fresh coriander
a little oil

1. Roughly chop the chickpeas and onions in a food processor.
2. Add the remaining ingredients, except the oil, and process until well mixed.
3. Heat a little oil in a non-stick frying pan and drop in spoonfuls of the mixture. Fry until golden-brown on one side, then flip over and fry on the other side. Drain on paper towel.

MAKES 12 BURGERS

Sweet and sour vegetable stir-fry

750 ml (3 cups) cooked brown basmati rice
a little olive oil
250 g button mushrooms
3 carrots, peeled and sliced
4 courgettes, sliced
1 bunch spring onions, sliced
6 baby corn, split in ½ lengthwise
50 ml toasted sesame seeds

DRESSING
10 ml (2 tsp) crushed garlic
10 ml (2 tsp) grated fresh ginger
½ pineapple, peeled and diced
grated rind of 1 lemon
45 ml (3 Tbsp) vinegar
30 ml (2 Tbsp) honey

1. Fry the rice in a wok in a little olive oil. Remove from the wok and set aside.
2. Fry the vegetables in the wok in batches until cooked, setting aside and adding more oil as necessary.
3. To make the dressing, combine all the ingredients and mix well.
4. Return the rice and vegetables to the wok to reheat, then pour over the dressing and sprinkle with the sesame seeds. Toss well before serving.

SERVES 6

Chickpea fritters

Brinjal and chickpea curry

This is one of my favourite dishes to make when I have a bumper crop of brinjals from my garden – Jenny.

30 ml (2 Tbsp) olive oil
1 onion, chopped
10 ml (2 tsp) chopped fresh garlic
10 ml (2 tsp) chopped fresh ginger
1–2 red chillies, deseeded and chopped
10 ml (2 tsp) garam masala
10 ml (2 tsp) ground coriander
10 ml (2 tsp) ground cumin
5 ml (1 tsp) turmeric
1 stick cinnamon
2 star anise
2–3 brinjals, diced
1 x 400 ml can lite coconut milk
1 x 410 g can chopped and peeled tomatoes
1 x 400 g can chickpeas, drained and rinsed
salt and freshly ground black pepper to taste
50 ml chopped fresh coriander

5. Heat the oil in a saucepan and gently fry the onion, garlic, ginger and chillies until the onion is soft. Add the spices and fry for a further 1 minute.
6. Add the brinjals, coconut milk, tomatoes and chickpeas, cover and simmer for 25–30 minutes until thick and saucy.
7. Season and add the coriander before serving with basmati rice.

SERVES 4

Lentil bobotie

This is a favourite classic dish with a twist. It's worth taking the time to fry the onions slowly as this will bring out the sweetness in them.

30 ml (2 Tbsp) olive oil
2 red onions, chopped
10 ml (2 tsp) chopped fresh garlic
15–20 ml (3–4 tsp) medium curry powder
2 slices brown bread, soaked in water for 10 minutes
2 x 400 g cans lentils, drained and rinsed
15 ml (1 Tbsp) white wine vinegar
15 ml (1 Tbsp) apricot jam
salt and freshly ground black pepper to taste
2 eggs
160 ml buttermilk or milk
3 ml (½ tsp) turmeric
6–8 bay leaves
a few slivered almonds

1. Heat the oil in a saucepan and gently fry the onions until soft. Add the garlic and cook for 1 minute, then add the curry powder and cook for a further minute until fragrant.
2. Squeeze out the excess water from the bread and add the bread to the saucepan, together with the lentils, vinegar and jam. Mix well and season to taste.
3. Transfer the mixture to an ovenproof casserole and smooth over the top.
4. Preheat the oven to 160 °C.
5. Combine the eggs, buttermilk or milk and turmeric in a jug and season well with salt and pepper.
6. Pour the egg-mixture over the bobotie, spike with the bay leaves and scatter over the almonds.
7. Bake for 20–30 minutes or until the topping is set. Serve with yellow rice, chutney and sliced banana.

SERVES 4

Mushroom and courgette frittata

Frittatas are very versatile and you can basically add any leftover from your fridge to them. Just make sure your pan is not too wide and the frittata too thin; a smaller, deeper pan is best.

30 ml (2 Tbsp) olive oil
1 red onion, chopped
30 g butter
250 g mushrooms, sliced
4 small courgettes, sliced
10 ml (2 tsp) chopped fresh garlic
8 eggs, beaten
salt and freshly ground black pepper to taste
125 ml (½ cup) grated cheese
a handful of fresh wild rocket
1 large avocado, peeled and sliced

1. Heat the oil in a 25 cm non-stick frying pan and fry the onion until soft.
2. Add the butter, mushrooms, courgettes and garlic and fry until cooked.
3. Pour over the beaten eggs, add salt and pepper to taste, and sprinkle over the cheese. Cook over medium heat until most of the mixture has set.
4. Preheat the oven's grill, then place the pan under the grill until the top of the frittata is puffed and golden.
5. Remove from the oven and slide onto a plate. Cut into four portions and top each with wild rocket and sliced avocado. Serve immediately.

Note: Vary the frittata by adding a variety of ingredients, such as bacon, ham, peppers, courgettes, roasted butternut and even cooked chicken or fish. It's always nice to serve the frittata with fresh rocket or baby salad leaves on top for a contrast in texture and heat.

SERVES 4

Leek and asparagus bake

This is a quick and easy dish using store-cupboard ingredients.

45 ml (3 Tbsp) olive oil
2 leeks, washed and finely sliced
30 ml (2 Tbsp) chopped fresh thyme
1 x 430 g can asparagus salad cuts, drained
1 x 410 g can whole kernel corn
125 ml (½ cup) grated Cheddar cheese
4 extra-large eggs
30 ml (2 Tbsp) cake flour
125 ml (½ cup) cream
250 ml (1 cup) milk
salt and freshly ground black pepper to taste

1. Heat the oil in a saucepan and fry the leeks and thyme over low heat for 10 minutes.
2. Preheat the oven to 180 °C. Grease a 23 cm ovenproof dish.
3. Put the leeks, asparagus and corn into the dish and sprinkle over the Cheddar cheese.
4. Whisk the eggs, flour, cream and milk together, season with salt and pepper, and pour over the leeks and asparagus.
5. Bake for 30–40 minutes or until set and lightly golden-brown. Serve with a mixed salad and garlic bread.

SERVES 4–6

Herb and mushroom pot pies

30 ml (2 Tbsp) olive oil
60 g butter
2 leeks, washed and sliced
5 ml (1 tsp) crushed garlic
150 g baby fennel, chopped
750 g mixed mushrooms, roughly chopped
15 ml (1 Tbsp) chopped fresh thyme
30 ml (2 Tbsp) chopped fresh parsley
100 ml dry white wine
250 g crème fraîche
salt and freshly ground black pepper to taste
1 x 400 g roll puff pastry, thawed
flour for rolling
1 egg, beaten

1. Heat the oil and butter in a heavy-based saucepan over medium heat and cook the leeks and garlic for 2 minutes until soft.
2. Add the fennel and cook for a further few minutes, then stir in the mushrooms and cook, tossing, until soft.
3. Add the herbs and wine and cook until the wine evaporates.
4. Stir in the crème fraîche, season to taste and remove from the heat. Spoon the mixture into four large, individual ovenproof dishes or ramekins and allow to cool.
5. Preheat the oven to 200 °C.
6. Lightly roll out the pastry on a floured work surface with a rolling pin to smooth out any creases. Cut out four circles large enough to fit on top of the dishes. Moisten the edges of the pastry circles with water, position on top of the dishes and press down to seal.
7. Using a sharp knife, make a slit in the centre of each pie, brush with the beaten egg and bake for 20 minutes or until the pastry is puffed and golden.

SERVES 4

Cheesy vegetable bake

60 g butter, softened
15 ml (1 Tbsp) chopped fresh thyme
30 ml (2 Tbsp) chopped fresh parsley
10 ml (2 tsp) crushed garlic
500 g potatoes, peeled and thinly sliced
salt and freshly ground black pepper to taste
500 g butternut, peeled and thinly sliced
1 red onion, thinly sliced
250 g courgettes, thinly sliced
250 ml (1 cup) tomato passata
125 ml (½ cup) grated Parmesan cheese

1. Preheat the oven to 160 °C. Grease a 1.5 litre ovenproof dish.
2. Combine the butter, thyme, parsley and garlic.
3. Place the potatoes onto the base of the dish and spread a third of the butter mixture over them. Season with salt and pepper.
4. Arrange the butternut and onion on top of the potatoes and spread with another third of the butter mixture. Season with salt and pepper.
5. Finish off with a layer of courgettes and the remaining butter mixture.
6. Spread the passata evenly over the top, cover and bake for 45 minutes.
7. Uncover and sprinkle over the Parmesan cheese. Return to the oven and bake uncovered for a further 15 minutes until golden-brown. Serve with focaccia to mop up the sauce.

SERVES 4

side dishes

Fruity couscous

125 ml (½ cup) orange juice
350 ml chicken stock
250 g couscous
15 ml (1 Tbsp) olive oil
1 red pepper, deseeded and finely chopped
1 yellow pepper, deseeded and finely chopped
1 red onion, finely chopped
6 spring onions, chopped
125 ml (½ cup) cranberries or raisins
a handful of fresh mint, chopped
salt and freshly ground black pepper to taste

1. Bring the orange juice and chicken stock to the boil in a large saucepan.
2. Add the couscous, remove from the heat, cover and leave to stand for 10 minutes.
3. Once the couscous has swelled, toss through the olive oil to loosen the grains and allow to cool.
4. Transfer to a serving bowl, add the remaining ingredients and toss through with a fork.

SERVES 8

Pasta rice salad

½ x 500 g pack pasta rice
125 g cocktail tomatoes, halved
½ cucumber, deseeded and diced
125 g mozzarella cheese, cubed
a bunch of spring onions, finely chopped
100 g black olives, pitted and halved
125 ml (½ cup) chopped fresh basil leaves or coriander

DRESSING
80 ml (⅓ cup) olive oil
45 ml (3 Tbsp) lemon juice
1 clove garlic, crushed
salt and freshly ground black pepper to taste

1. Cook the pasta rice according to package instructions, drain immediately and rinse well under cold water. Watch carefully, as pasta rice can overcook very quickly.
2. To make the dressing, combine all the ingredients and mix well.
3. Place the rice in a bowl with the remaining salad ingredients and pour over the dressing. Toss and serve.

SERVES 4–6

Cauliflower 'rice'

This is a great substitute for rice. It has a similar texture and quite a neutral flavour, and is ideal with curries and stews if you are trying to cut down on starch.

500 g cauliflower
30 ml (2 Tbsp) olive oil
1–2 cloves garlic, crushed
1 onion, finely chopped
salt and freshly ground black pepper to taste

1. Process the cauliflower, including the core, in a food processor until crumbly.
2. Heat the oil in a large frying pan and sauté the garlic and onion until tender.
3. Add the cauliflower and cook, stirring, until light golden-brown. Season to taste.

SERVES 4

Yellow rice

We learned how to make this rice from one of our favourite cooks, Ina Paarman. It goes really well with bobotie.

250 ml (1 cup) rice
625 ml (2½ cups) water
5 ml (1 tsp) salt
10 ml (2 tsp) turmeric
1 stick cinnamon
125 ml (½ cup) raisins
30 ml (2 Tbsp) honey
30 g butter

1. Boil the rice in the water with the salt and turmeric for 15–20 minutes until cooked. Drain and put the rice in a colander over a pot of simmering water.
2. Add the cinnamon stick and raisins and steam for 5 minutes until the rice is fluffy.
3. Tip into a serving bowl, remove the cinnamon stick and fork through the honey and butter.

SERVES 4

Roasted vegetables

250 g butternut, cut into medium-sized chunks
3–4 courgettes, cut into 2 cm pieces
125 g patty pans, halved
2 onions, cut into wedges
1 red pepper, deseeded and cut into pieces
1 yellow pepper, deseeded and cut into pieces
1 brinjal, cubed
salt and black pepper to taste
45 ml (3 Tbsp) olive oil
a bunch of mixed fresh herbs, roughly chopped (basil, thyme, parsley, etc.)
a pinch of sugar
250 g mushrooms, halved
200 g baby tomatoes
15 ml (1 Tbsp) balsamic vinegar

1. Preheat the oven to 180 °C.
2. Place all of the vegetables, except the mushrooms and tomatoes, in a single layer on a baking tray or ovenproof dish. Season with salt and pepper.
3. Combine the oil, herbs and sugar and drizzle over the vegetables, then toss to coat.
4. Roast for 15–20 minutes, then mix in the mushrooms and tomatoes and cook for a further 15 minutes or until the vegetables are tender.
5. Remove from the oven, season with salt and pepper and drizzle over the balsamic vinegar before serving.

SERVES 6

Crushed Parmesan potatoes

500 g potatoes, peeled
250 ml (1 cup) milk
250 ml (1 cup) water
a large pinch of salt
30 g butter
15 ml (1 Tbsp) olive oil
45 ml (3 Tbsp) cream
30 ml (2 Tbsp) grated Parmesan cheese
15 ml (1 Tbsp) chopped fresh parsley

1. Put the potatoes, milk, water and salt in a medium saucepan and bring to the boil. Cook for 20–25 minutes until the potatoes are soft. Drain off the liquid, leaving about 30 ml (2 Tbsp) in the pan.
2. Add the butter and crush lightly with a potato masher.
3. Add the olive oil and cream and carefully fold into the potatoes.
4. Preheat the oven's grill. Grease an ovenproof dish.
5. Spoon the potatoes into the dish and sprinkle over the Parmesan cheese and parsley.
6. Place under the grill for a few minutes until lightly golden-brown.

SERVES 4–6

Potato wedges

Vary the flavour by replacing the lemon juice and rosemary with a spice rub or even a curry paste such as harissa.

4 large potatoes, cut into wedges, peeled or unpeeled if the skins are nice
50 ml olive oil
25 ml (5 tsp) lemon juice
salt and freshly ground black pepper to taste
15 ml (1 Tbsp) chopped fresh rosemary

1. Preheat the oven to 200 °C.
2. Boil the potatoes in a large saucepan of water for about 10 minutes. Drain well and put into an oven roasting pan.
3. Combine the olive oil, lemon juice, seasoning and rosemary and pour over the potatoes. Toss well to coat.
4. Roast for 20–30 minutes until golden and crispy.

SERVES 4

Perfect mash

4 medium potatoes, peeled and chopped
5 ml (1 tsp) salt
30 g butter
50–60 ml warm milk
salt and freshly ground black pepper to taste

1. Place the potatoes into a saucepan and cover with water. Add the salt, cover and boil for 20–30 minutes until the potatoes are soft but not disintegrated. Drain off the water, and then return the pan to the heat to cook off any excess water.
2. Add the butter and milk and mash using a potato masher or ricer until no lumps remain. Season well with salt and pepper, and serve immediately.

SERVES 4

Cheesy potato and broccoli mash

4 potatoes, peeled and cubed
1 x 300 g punnet tender stem broccoli, roughly chopped
80 ml (⅓ cup) warm milk
30 g butter
125 ml (½ cup) grated Cheddar cheese
salt and freshly ground black pepper to taste

1. Boil the potatoes and broccoli in a saucepan of water until soft. Drain.
2. Add the milk, butter and Cheddar cheese.
3. Mash well, season to taste and serve.

SERVES 4

Spiced sweet potato mash

If orange sweet potatoes are not available, use butternut.

500 g orange sweet potatoes
45 ml (3 Tbsp) brown sugar
30 g butter
5 ml (1 tsp) grated orange rind
30 ml (2 Tbsp) orange juice
3 ml (½ tsp) ground cinnamon
3 ml (½ tsp) ground allspice
a pinch of grated nutmeg
salt and freshly ground black pepper to taste

1. Boil the sweet potatoes in a saucepan of water until soft. Drain.
2. Add the sugar, butter, orange rind, orange juice and spices. Season to taste.
3. Mash using a potato masher or purée in a blender until smooth.

SERVES 4

Butterbean mash

This is a great substitute for potato mash if you are trying to add fibre to a meal. The added bonus is that it's so quick to make.

45 ml (3 Tbsp) olive oil
10 ml (2 tsp) chopped fresh garlic
2 x 410 g cans butterbeans, drained
10 ml (2 tsp) chopped fresh rosemary
salt and freshly ground black pepper to taste

1. Heat the oil in a small saucepan and gently fry the garlic for 1–2 minutes.
2. Add the butterbeans and rosemary and cook for 2–3 minutes to infuse the flavours. Season to taste.
3. Mash with a potato masher or stick blender until creamy, adding more olive oil if necessary.

SERVES 4

Recipe index

Conversion chart

METRIC	US CUPS	IMPERIAL
3 ml	½ tsp	–
5 ml	1 tsp	3/16 fl oz
15 ml	1 Tbsp	½ fl oz
25 ml	5 tsp	1 fl oz
60 ml	4 Tbsp	2 fl oz
80 ml	⅓ cup	2 ¾ fl oz
125 ml	½ cup	4 fl oz
180 ml	¾ cup	7 fl oz
250 ml	1 cup	9 fl oz
25 g	–	1 oz
50 g	–	2 oz
75 g	–	3 oz
100 g	–	4 oz
150 g	–	5 oz
200 g	–	7 oz
250 g	–	9 oz
500 g	–	1 lb 2 oz
750 g	–	1 lb 10 oz
1 kg	–	2 lb 4 oz

Oven Temperatures

°C (Celsius)	°F (Fahrenheit)	GAS MARK
100 °C	200 °F	¼
110 °C	225 °F	¼
120 °C	250 °F	½
140 °C	275 °F	1
150 °C	300 °F	2
160 °C	325 °F	3
180 °C	350 °F	4
190 °C	375 °F	5
200 °C	400 °F	6
220 °C	425 °F	7
230 °C	450 °F	8
240 °C	475 °F	9